This Mo

This Month We Celebrate
Ann Easter

Collins
Fount Paperbacks

William Collins Sons & Co. Ltd
London · Glasgow · Sydney · Auckland
Toronto · Johannesburg

First published in Great Britain in 1990 by Fount Paperbacks

Fount Paperbacks is an imprint of
Collins Religious Division,
part of the Collins Publishing Group
8 Grafton Street, London W1X 3LA

Typeset by Avocet Robinson, Buckingham
Printed and bound in Great Britain by William Collins
Sons & Co. Ltd, Glasgow

Dedication

This book is dedicated to those many
people who, in their generous and
forgiving love for me, have shown me
something of the love of God, and thus
daily bolster my feeble faith

Contents

Introduction

Everyone experiences the "celebrations" that mark our passage through life, either individually or corporately. Whether it be the birthday or simply putting away winter clothes, New Year's Day or Fireworks Night, we notice the markers which indicate time's passing.

I think God gives us these celebrations so that we have an opportunity to explore a moment in time, to look back to the past and forward into the future. We have a chance to see where we've got to – some may rejoice, others bemoan the new step along the road of life. We look back and realize all that is no more, and inevitably, experience relief and loss, as we notice hurdles overcome and congratulate ourselves – at the time we probably thought we'd never make it, yet somehow we did. But we notice too the people and things that we never thought we'd miss – maybe a home or a job, or a way of life that, though it had its problems (what doesn't!) was comforting in its familiarity.

Looking forward is exciting for some people, especially perhaps the young, but I know that many face the future with dread. For some people there is every reason so to do, but for others it is the fear of the unknown, and a desire for certainty, that makes them worry about what's to come.

And it is into the midst of this peculiar human state, with our regrets and congratulations, our hopes and our fears, that God throws the disruptive spanner of a special occasion. And, having thrown the spanner, God is there to help us to use it, the celebration, to reveal something of God to us, and to reveal something of ourselves to us too.

By pausing in that God-given moment, we can, in our turmoil and unknowing, get a feel of God – a hidden shape to the world, a plan, only fragments of which are glimpsed, which can reassure us that, no matter what the future may bring, God will be there with us, loving us, and longing for us to notice the presence of the Holy Spirit in our lives.

One
January – New Year

Everybody has a new start on 1st January. A new year with all its seasons and anniversaries. A chance for improvement on last year and a new number to write on letters and cheques.

Perhaps the year is our most impressive recurring cyclical change marker, the very term "anniversary", although not always talking about something once a year, is our most popular word for this sort of celebration. A year, after all, contains all the extremes – the longest and the shortest days; the coldest and the hottest days; the garden bursting with colour, and later seeming almost dead. Although some plants flourish twice in a year, most flowers fruit and seed just once. A month, or even a season, can't compete with those differences, and a decade has too many.

Our lives are measured by years, not seasons or decades – though somehow "in her thirties" sounds more positive than "age thirty-nine" – but the new year is a marker that we can all share, unlike our birthdays.

So we embark together on this new segment, accompanied on TV by all sorts of Scots people who have at any time been anything remotely famous, and cheered by an extra statutory day on which to go to the sales, only to find all the presents we bought

13

before Christmas reduced to half-price. Since all of the United Kingdom now has this Bank Holiday, should we perhaps skip the Scottish element? – but what would we put in its place? I notice that a "God-slot" has been slipped in on TV in recent years – perhaps an indication of our corporate recognition of time's running away ever faster – or maybe it's that as modern life becomes more violent and frightening, people feel they need a prayer, and the acknowledgement of God to help them through the year to come. Of course, Watch Night services are an old tradition, so maybe it's a throwback to them.

Not that anybody would go to church on New Year's Eve, though! We are all supposed to be bopping the night away, at least passively, with our wee friends on the Box. I wonder if some of us are frightened to put too much emphasis on this particular marker? We firmly assert that we "don't bother with that sort of thing", then go home and lie awake in the dark listening as the clock strikes midnight and ushers in a New Year.

What will it be like? More of the same? Grief, Loneliness, Suffering? Will it be a struggle against time and age?

But could it perhaps be a New Start? Could it be a clean slate?

The truth is that it cannot. The slates of our lives are already marked indelibly with the successes and failures, loves and hates, hopes and fears that we have sustained so far, and although we might wish to rub out the pain and the scars, we know that they help to determine the person we are.

But, in the Baptism Service we do talk about a new birth, and although that couldn't be an attraction for one recently born, the idea of a new start might be the essence of a request for adult baptism.

I once asked a lady why she wanted her baby son to be baptized. She assured me that she knew it was the right thing to do, because she remembered seeing *photographs* of Jesus doing it! Some say that a baby doesn't begin to thrive until (s)he is christened; and it has become, for some people, a sort of rite of passage, a hurdle to be jumped in order to secure good fortune for the child.

But I try to see it a bit like soap powders. Once upon a time, you could advertise "*New*" Soapo, or whatever, and it was actually the old one in a new box, but these days, trades descriptions acts have made us say "*New Improved*" Soapo, and surely that's how it is with us. We're not going to be new and different; we cannot start again, like Nicodemus, asking to be returned to our mother's womb. Rather, baptism affirms our place in God's family and affections, and gives us the chance to be "Improved".

What makes those tea advertisement chimpanzees funny is that they're aping (sorry!) humans by wearing clothes and seeming to speak, which is all right for fun, but no good for a way of life. God wants us to be the best Thomasina, Dick or Harry that we can be, and gives us the grace to do it with outward, visible signs like baptism. It is meant as an opportunity for a new start, as indeed is each and every day, but it's another episode of our life journey, not a new book.

In the baptism service people first make a decision, a statement of their intended goal, their aim to turn to Christ, repent of their sins and renounce evil. But we recognize that to be an aim, rather than an achievement – something which we can attempt, but which will not be perfected until we get to Heaven. So we mark our intention towards this goal with a badge, a cross, signed on the forehead. Of course, it immediately disappears – staying only slightly longer if made in oil of chrism (hence "christening") – but remains an invisible reminder of our aim.

When I was a teenager on my first visit abroad, I couldn't understand how everyone knew immediately that I was English, and I said that it was as if I had written across my forehead – "I am ENGLISH". Would that others would recognize our faith so quickly, from our behaviour and our tone of speech – but each of us baptized has that unseen badge for evermore.

Then there's the water itself. It wasn't a new idea that Jesus invented; rather he took an old idea and made it holy. People had been dipped in water as a symbol of regeneration and cleansing for years. I suppose too that in the Middle East, water was that much more precious, so the symbolism attached to washing was rather more special than today. Royal babies have water specially flown from the River Jordan, and perhaps it has thus been through the system fewer times than the tap water I use in the East End of London! But I'm quite sure that, just as blessing it affirms that ordinary old water as the water of eternal life for those to be baptized in it, so in baptizing, God affirms that, even in our mucky old sinful state, we are children of God, and heirs of grace.

But before the water is poured, a way forward

must be indicated. It's all very well to decide on and declare goals, but our immediate need is the way forward now. We have decided on our life's destination – which route shall we take? And that question is answered by faith; belief and trust in the one God, Father, Son and Holy Spirit, and it's that will get us there in the end.

It is at this point that the minister asks for the name in which the person is to be baptized. I usually say, "Name this Child", and as a rule that obtains the desired reply, but once I said it to the much qualified solicitor godfather of a child, who replied, "Yes please"! When I repeated the request, adding quietly, "William John", he said loudly, 'Yes, that's right". I tried again, a little more firmly, and at last the man smiled broadly and said, "Yes, that's right. Name this child William John". We got there in the end.

Then the water is poured. I always like to make the babe's head really wet, so that when I put the baby back upright, water drips down its face – they don't usually complain, just wonder what on earth is going on.

My friend in the next parish actually sits the child in the font and encourages it to play with the water. My friend is a bachelor. My experience of bathing my own babies would make me feel that this baptism method has definite disaster potential.

Then the one being baptized, or a representative, is handed a lighted candle, representing passing from darkness to light as the truth of faith and God's love begins to dawn on us. And the final activity is the welcome. Some congregations applaud, which is quite fun, but in church I like to try to keep to things that people do naturally, so I usually carry the baby, or lead the child, into the middle of the congregation so that they all go "aaah!" − it never fails.

This is a good reason for having baptisms at the main service in church. How can a person be welcomed officially by the congregation when the congregation isn't there? Of course, in the old days, many more people did attend church, so any family group would probably include several church members, but these days one is often welcoming the whole family, actually, and so it's nice to have some church members there to do that. The problem with this idea, though, is that it then leaves the hapless parents with an assortment of family and friends hanging about halfway through Sunday morning, when often most of them would normally still be in bed reading the papers. However, most families I have known have coped with the unusual hour, and have then spent the rest of the day welcoming the baby into their family, and enjoying themselves together.

In the Church of England the service of infant baptism begins with the godparents agreeing to bring up the child as a Christian and to help and encourage it to come to confirmation, which is, as it were, the other half of the original initiation ceremony. In it the candidates, who have usually undergone some sort of learning in preparation, make their baptismal vows for themselves, in front of a bishop, who then puts his hands onto their head, to confirm them with the Holy Spirit. It is the touch which is all-important, being passed down through the ages directly from Our Lord.

There is no doubt that a lot of Jesus's ministry

was through direct physical contact. He often laid hands on people to heal them. Jesus took Jairus's daughter by the hand, when it was thought that she was dead. He spat on the ground and made clay of the spittle and anointed the blind man's eyes (John 9:6); they brought children that Jesus should touch them (Mark 10:13). Some of these things seem a bit "physical" to our English minds, and therefore slightly unpleasant – perhaps our natures are a bit reserved and cannot cope with the more effusive Middle Eastern way. I think the fact that, until fairly recently, almost all ministers of religion were male may have something to do with it. Watch a bishop confirming a row of youngsters. He will touch their heads rather gingerly, as if worried about disturbing their hair-dos. This is where being a woman minister makes things easier – and there aren't many situations when you can say that!

When I first went to the little church in London's East End, the congregation was so small that we shared the cubs' Christmas party, but the next year the congregation had grown, so we had a little tea party of our own. It went so well, and I was delighted when an elderly lady, who was a widow, with no children, thanked me for organizing the party, and said that she had thoroughly enjoyed it. I was so pleased that I grabbed the lady by the sholders and kissed her on both cheeks. I was a bit taken aback and wondered if I'd done the right thing (or indeed, if I was standing on her foot), when tears came into her eyes. But I realized later that, given her situation, it was maybe years since she had been kissed.

Since then, I have tried to take opportunities

19

though not, I think, in a contrived way — to touch people. After a funeral I conducted for a young man who'd had Down's Syndrome, his friends from the adult training centre all kissed me solemnly as they left the chapel. There was no self-consciousness about it — unlike some congregations at "the Peace" in a Communion Service, when people look around uneasily, wondering who is next going to accost them with a "meaningful" handshake!

Ideally, a touch should be a natural blessing, reinforced by words rather than the other way around. It's a shame that the handshake is not so popular now as a form of greeting, as that was an easy way to give someone the warmth of touch even if you didn't know them so well. We all need to be touched — experiments have shown that baby monkeys, given all the other necessities of life but no opportunity to touch, stroke or cuddle another body, will not thrive. It is part of our so-called civilized British society that we do not feel able to invade each other's "body-space", and yet I find it quite uncivilized that people who are alone, like my lady at St James's, have no opportunity to touch or be touched.

A New Year gives us an opportunity to fan the glowing embers of our faith, warmed and encouraged as they have been by the festival of Christmas, and vow to be, in our own selves, more of the whole person that God wants us to be.

Two
February – Valentine's Day

Christmas and New Year are almost forgotten and the last candle of Candlemas has been put away when, right in the middle of cold, dark February, God gives us a silly, frilly opportunity to celebrate romantic love on St Valentine's Day. There seems to be no connection between the third-century martyr and courting couples, except perhaps a rather tenuous suggestion that birds are supposed to pair on 14th February.

But, encouraged by the card manufacturers and gift shops, this day has become a festival of romantic love, an opportunity for marriage proposals and "anonymous" declarations of affection. Cards saying "I Love You" are available in every type of artistic style and addressed to everyone – mothers, fathers, friends. Perhaps it's a shame that we should need a contrived occasion to tell people that we love them, but Valentine's Day can jog the memory, and give a ready-shaped opportunity to say something that we know we feel, but don't often say out loud.

Valentine's Day is most observed when it falls on a Friday or Saturday when, as well as "disco-luv-ins" and Valentine's Day Fancy Dress Balls, lots of people make the most of the festival and get engaged or married.

It is said that these days there are more weddings

than ever before, and certainly, more money is spent on the festivities by more people. Preparations start years in advance, to secure the right time of day at the right church, and, more important, the right venue for the reception. Special outfits for the wedding party – two for some of them – are bought or made, and, if it's to be a proper "sit-down", the tricky question of who sits next to whom, and how near the top of the table, becomes much more important than the question of what will be eaten. Friends are delighted or offended to be invited or otherwise, and pity the bride with lots of friends with young children, all of whom are offered as attendants. Does she choose them all, and chance being upstaged by their cuteness, not to mention their cheeky antics, or does she choose just one or two and risk offending all the other mothers and grandmothers?

The latest innovation is the video film, so that, as the day dawns and the bride rushes around in her underclothes looking for a hanky and her "going-away" shoes, she can be sure of being filmed for posterity. But then the vintage car or landau and pony or beribboned limousine arrives, and off she goes. At the church, her anxious groom awaits, having arrived in good time. Of course, his "stag night" celebrations now take place several days before the wedding to allow complete recovery. The groom is wished luck and encouraged by long-forgotten distant members of his family, until they are all required to extinguish their cigarettes and ushered into church by the verger, who conspicu-ously eyes the cigarette ends smouldering amongst the last lot's confetti and reminds himself of the whereabouts of the fire-extinguisher just in case. The books are in position in the pews, though the verger doubts that they will be used – unlike the very large brass collection plate by the door, which he will shuffle loudly to make quite sure that it is used.

The air of expectancy heightens as the bridesmaids arrive and (usually) shiver in their off-the-shoulder dresses as their photgraphs are taken, and then, the long-awaited arrival of the bride and her father, and the slow glide up the aisle.

As a minister, I have only recently been able to conduct weddings, and I have found those first bars of the Bridal March, or whatever, a very emotional moment. It is terribly moving, ignoring all the mad activity going on around them, to witness two people making life-long vows to each other, and I have often had to steel myself to carry on when my heart has lurched at a glance or a hand-squeeze between them that says it all. Those who, at the rehearsal, giggled and confessed their inability to concentrate, are suddenly riveted to a moment when time has stopped, and their love is formally bound in God's love, as their hands are linked and wrapped in my stole.

At that moment there is a visible release of tension as everyone realizes that it's happened and their couple are married. There remains only for the minister to make sure that the correct signatures get into the right places in the registers, and the restless congregation are released into their orgy of photography, food and drink.

With all the extras which seem now to be obligatory, it seems amazing that God would ever be felt at a wedding which is the epitome of materialism, but, somehow, God manages it. After all, it was at a wedding that Jesus was revealed as something more than an ordinary man, and I think that God continues to make basic elements of man and woman, tired and cynical though they are, into the heady new wine of a marriage partnership. For underneath the struggle to find right outfits, organize the reception and sort out a home, there is a new knot in the net of our community which is being formed at a wedding, and the efforts, maybe misguided, to make the wedding sensational, are surely actually the embodiment of the desire of the community to get this new unit off the ground and into the future, so that our future as a group is assured.

What we wear at a wedding, especially where I live in the East End of London, is of critical importance, and many hundreds of pounds are spent on special outfits. So I was delighted to hear that the Koran says that husband and wife should be like garments for each other. What a lovely idea, for what could be closer to us than our clothes, what could be more special than our wedding outfit?

But more than that, clothes perform vital functions in our lives that marriage partners do well to imitate. Clothes protect us from the elements – cold, dampness and occasionally, the heat, just as our partner protects us from the world and some of its troubles. Once a couple are married it's you-and-me against the world, and a loving partner can do much to help us through the cold reality of some parts of life, the dampness of depression, grief and disappointment, and the heat of too much to do. When life is going badly, God gives us our partner to soothe and cheer, and to commiserate with the discomfort. When we feel down, what better than someone very close to share the fog of depression which clouds our vision and makes our heart heavy. And when the pace of life gets too fast, it is a truly loving thing to stand in front of our partner, and say "No more", when perhaps they themselves haven't realized how stressed things have become. These days we can get caught up so easily in hectic activity, because so much is on offer. The whole world is available to be tasted and tried, not to mention the "fulfilment" that we are told we must all obtain, through our work, our hobbies, our families and our sex lives.

Then, our clothes are chosen to be appropriate, to make us feel right, so that we are confident and can stand up straight. For months and even years before the wedding, couples ponder on whether this partner is appropriate for them. "Does (s)he make me feel confident and proud of myself, or does (s)he make me cringe with embarrassment, or shrink with fear?" At its best, marriage is a growth point, not just for the newly-formed unit, but for each of the couple as individuals. With a new security, and extra confidence gained from the knowledge that someone knows them very well and still wants to spend the rest of their lives with them, people experience a certain liberation, perhaps rather different from the idea of "settling down" that others talk about. The old song said, "Stay as sweet as you are", but actually, that's the last thing that should happen. The hope is that people will not only remain as sweet, but in fact become sweeter as they learn more about themselves, each other, love and life. Some people, especially women, believe that they must give up all outside interests and friends when they get married. I think that that is sad, as it means that they have nothing new and refreshing to bring to the relationship. Better to retain a certain amount of independence, so that the choice to spend time with one's partner becomes a real decision – rather than there being no one and nothing else!

And our clothes, in being appropriate, make us feel comfortable. At the wedding, we are dressed in special new clothes and perhaps new shoes. I remember once attending a cousin's wedding and kneeling down behind four of my aunts, all of whom still had the price labels on their new shoes! At another, typically East End wedding, several of the women guests had brought fluffy bedroom slippers with them, which looked most peculiar with their wedding finery when they put them on during the reception. But, even if we don't bring them to the wedding, where would we be without our sloppy cardigans and our old slippers? We all need clothes in which we can relax completely, just as we need relationships in which we can be absolutely ourselves, without feeling that we need to put on an act as a shield to hide behind. In the best sort of marriage partnership, each partner is free to be entirely her- or himself, and in that freedom can discover things about self, partner and perhaps even God.

Ideally, not only will the two involved learn about God's love, but others around them, especially their children, will feel something of the warmth of the love that is shared, because surely the partnership which protects, nurtures and comforts, is a sign of

God's grace and a gift which, like all good gifts, shows us something of the giver.

However, there is no denying that one of the reasons why there are more weddings these days is that people get married more than once. I believe that this has a lot to do with the fact that people live longer. The average marriage in early Victorian times lasted about fourteen years, because so many of the marriages were ended by an industrial accident, death in childbirth, or disease. I've no doubt that sometimes the mourning was tinged with relief as unhappy liaisons were ended, as well as the blissful ones. So what nature once did for us, the divorce courts do now.

I really don't believe that people don't try so hard, rather that, given the above simple sociological/ health reasons, the whole pattern of marriage has changed. The significance of child-bearing and rearing has assumed a much less important place in people's lives because of effective contraception. My grandmother was around forty when she gave birth to her sixth child, which meant that the greatest part of her middle years were taken up with her children. Fifty years later, my friend Christine had two boys within thirteen months of each other when she was in her early twenties, and returned to work when the younger was three years old, so she only spent a small part of her life as a full-time mother and housewife. By the time she was forty, perhaps halfway through her life, Christine's sons were away at college and very much off her hands.

Christine was quite unusual, in that her in-laws lived only five minutes' drive away, and often visited and helped with childcare. So many people these days move miles away from their families, in order to buy their own home, or because of their jobs, and do not enjoy the support of their family as my grandmother did. She, on the Isle of Dogs, in East London, had her mother and mother-in-law, sisters, cousins and aunts, all within easy walking distance. When a child was fractious there was always someone to offer advice, or take him out for an hour, and if my grandfather was "unco-operative" or difficult, there were women all around to support her and sympathize.

But perhaps the most important factor in the changing pattern of marriage is the "liberation" of women, not only liberation from constant pregnancies, but liberation into the expectation of fulfilment of emotional needs as well as being free to pursue a career. Women are educated to believe that they can do, or be, anything they want. Professional careers (with certain notable ecclesiastical exceptions) are open to them; they expect to have money of their own, and freedom to spend it as they wish. Women (and children) are no longer the chattels of men, and do not have to put up with violence or cruelty, as they no longer derive economic or social status solely from them.

Given the changing pattern of marriage, and the fact that nowadays one in three marriages ends in divorce, what should be the Church's response? It has been said that if we paid more attention to preparation for first marriages, our deliberations over second marriages would be unnecessary, but that's difficult when so often the first time the minister meets the couple, the decision has been made, and preparations for the wedding are well under way.

I have often mused on the possibility of changing the vows, but how could that be done without watering down the intention of the marriage commitment? Although it's not a popular choice, I would like to change to the continental system, where everyone is married in a registry office, but then those who wish it go to church for a blessing. That's what Christopher and I decided to do when we were married in 1987. Although several clergy friends would have been prepared to marry us – the problem being the dissolution of my previous marriage – we elected to be married, with just two of our friends as witnesses, in the local registry office. The Registrar was very concerned that, both being clerics, we might try to slip in a prayer somewhere, but he needn't have worried, as there was to be time and opportunity for that later when, after a meal with family and close friends, we all went to church for our nuptial mass.

The church was full of people, and the singing was wonderful, but it's not that that people remember, nor the thoughtful sermon or prayers, it's the PETALS.

Not long before our wedding, we'd attended a Greek Orthodox Easter service, where the priest threw white flower petals over the congregation. All the lights came on, and bells were rung, and, though I couldn't understand a word, my spine was tingling with the exhilaration. The sense of new life bursting out of the tomb was so vivid, and we decided that we must have petals at our wedding, to symbolize the new start and the joy of our love.

So, after the service had finished, the organist burst into a lively voluntary, and Christopher and I walked down the aisle showering our applauding, and rather surprised, friends with petals.

I am quite sure that there is much that the churches could do to support and heal some of the rifts in first marriages, but I believe that, given the changing patterns of married life outlined above, some marriages will inevitably die before the death of one of the partners. I don't think that anyone could take lightly the decision to marry a second time after the failure of the first, but when that happens, I believe that the churches should do what they can to help avoid a second failure which, sadly, is all too common.

Surely, the mark of true love is to forgive, and, if people feel, as so many do, that to have a second try at marriage is unforgivable, we miss the opportunity to assure them of God's presence in, and hopes for, their relationship.

Three
March – Mothering Sunday

Mothering Sunday usually occurs in March, though, being always the fourth Sunday in Lent, the actual date changes from year to year. It is said that the custom arose when youngsters in service, working away from home, were allowed a day off in early Spring to go to visit their families, and perhaps take a little present of flowers or a cake to their mother.

But, whatever the origin, the idea of a day when people can give a special thank you to and for their mother, is a good one. From morning sickness through to grandchildren's sickness, motherhood is demanding emotionally and physically, and we only begin to understand the demands that we made on our mothers when we become parents ourselves.

I worked for nine years as the assistant to the Chaplain at Newham General Hospital in East London, where I had responsibility for the maternity unit. I visited every week, and simply walked around in my cassock chatting to people, patients, their visitors and the staff. A churching (thanksgiving for the birth of a baby) service was advertised, and sometimes a Christian mother would ask me to pray with her and perhaps her husband. Sometimes a mother would say that her mother had said that she must be "done" before she left hospital — "And are you the lady that does it?" I often wondered what they expected to happen; they knew only that something mysterious would take place which would somehow bless the baby (with good luck, perhaps?) and render them fit to leave hospital.

But once I wandered around and looked into a cot where a simply beautiful African baby was sleeping. I tried to chat to his mother, but she seemed uninterested, until I turned to go, when she suddenly announced, "I'm going to call him 'Harry', do you think that's a good name?" I had to laugh, because my father's name is Harry, and no one could have been more different from the middle-aged European with thinning hair than the soot-black babe with his luxuriantly curly mop, in the cradle. I explained my amusement, and said that, if her baby grew up to be anything like my father, she would be pleased and proud. The mother told me that they had waited ten years for this baby, and that she couldn't find the right words to express her joy and thanks to God. Thus it was my enormous privilege to help that lady to find the words she wanted, and to share her tears of joy in the wonder of creation.

When you start a new job, you can give it up if you don't like it; if you go to Australia you can always come back, but when you have a baby your life is changed for ever, almost regardless of what happens to the baby. When Simeon told Our Lady, "A sword will pierce your soul also", he foretold the pain of motherhood, especially when the child dies. The "down" side of my job was that, occasionally, babies do die, sometimes for no apparent reason at all.

Sometimes I might reach the hospital in time to do an emergency baptism, and to gaze helplessly at the little soul as she struggled for life, encouraged and helped at every faltering breath by devoted staff, and her devastated parents. But sometimes the baby was stillborn, and had known life only within the womb. At these times I leaned heavily on the literature and personal support provided by the Stillbirth and Neo-Natal Death Society (SANDS). They recommended that as much of a memory be constructed as possible, so the parents hold their baby, and take photographs, and maybe have a lock of hair or the identity bracelet to keep. It is suggested that there should be a proper funeral service and perhaps an opportunity to erect a stone or record the baby's name in a book.

This part of my job was always difficult, but one family that I remember especially were the Holmeses. Sandie and Neil were a charming young couple, he a travel agent, she a teacher, and their first baby was much wanted and looked forward to. However, during a routine ante-natal visit, Sandie was told that no heart-beat could be detected. This isn't unusual – it's only a little heart after all – but further tests confirmed their worst fears: their baby had died.

In such a case, it is generally regarded as safest to await the baby's natural birth rather than to operate, but this particular baby took five days to be delivered, during which time, as you can imagine, Sandie and Neil sunk to the depths of grief. But they weren't alone – it seemed as if the whole hospital shared in their waiting, and even the porter at the hospital gate would ask me, "How's Sandie – any news?" But eventually, baby Joseph was born, quite perfect, and the flood of emotions washed over us all as he was held and washed and dressed later, in preparation for his funeral, a sad little service on a bright summer's day.

I'd like to tell you all the good points to this story, to tell you how Sandie and Neil recovered from the tragedy and went on to have two more lovely children; and how they were instrumental in running our local SANDS group. I'd like to tell you how their faith held them up and how everyone rallied round; that they tried to accept what had happened philosophically, and that it deepened their love for each other. Indeed, all those things are true, but then that might make you think that their faith made things easy to cope with, and that they felt no pain. But it didn't.

Sandie and Neil were angry – with God, with each other, with the hospital – with anybody. They railed against God and said, "Why us?" They argued logically that their relationship and their home would have been just right for a baby, unlike some others. There was despair, misery, tears, feelings of guilt and recriminations. Was there any way that little Joe could have been saved?

But no, faith certainly didn't mean a panacea; what it did mean was that, in the depths of what, at the time, seemed a totally negative experience, there was a glimpse of eternity, of God-with-us in the very centre of our pain and suffering. And in that glimpse, a real hope that, one day, somehow, little Joseph will be waiting for us. The spring flowers of Mothering Sunday glow amid the purple pall of Lent – motherhood is not all sweetness and light.

Yet it is exactly that side of the experience which makes me feel that perhaps there is something of the nature of God in mothering. Who loves us better than our mother? Whose patience and understanding, protectiveness and forgiveness could be more

38

generous than a mother's? Almost entirely throughout the animal kingdom, it is the mother who cares for the young, even, in the case of the pelican, feeding them with her own flesh. A mother is not afraid to be physically caught up with the children, from the sticky dampness of breast feeding, to the equally sticky dampness of washing sports gear and tending grazes and cuts.

My own mother is a prime example. She worked for most of my childhood to make sure that my sister and I could live in a nice home that was our own, have music lessons and go on school holidays abroad – all things which she herself had never had. She fought against the gradually paralysing effect of multiple sclerosis, although the easy-going side of her nature made her more inclined to accept what was happening. Now she is quite paralysed, depending upon others, principally my father, to do everything for her.

I think that her faith in God is perhaps one of the most profound and comprehensive that I know. When my sister and I were children, she often brought God into ordinary conversations without sounding at all pious or eccentric. "And what do you think God will say about THAT when you come to face him in Heaven?", she would demand if we tried to cheat or lie. "Remember that Jesus will be with you", she would say, comforting us when we were nervous or frightened. But don't think that our mother was "wet" – the auburn hair which runs in our family indicates a fiery temper, and we all delight to remind her of the time that she threw a cake-stand at my father! God is an immediate reality, to be taken into account at all times, and so I think that, as well as teaching us about God by her telling of stories and sending us to church, she also teaches us about God by her life, of which patience must be an essential keynote.

Some people object to the possibility of saying "Our Mother" as well as "Our Father", but I can see that as a useful motif, as certainly my mother demonstrates qualities which speak of God's love and put it into action. And I can understand how some people who haven't had much experience of a father's love could find the motif useful. After all, if your father hit or abused you, or left you, or was unnecessarily strict and harsh with you, what sort of image of God would you have? You might have a fantasy of a loving father, but the hard reality would still be there.

I think that the image of a mother-God is a warm, cuddling, all-forgiving love which all of us need sometimes, and I am happy to use it as one of God's faces. But I'm sure that God is bigger than any mother or father.

To use a feminine image of God, as does the Bible on occasions (Isaiah 49:14−15; 66:13; Matthew 23:37) is not to diminish God − rather, I think, it helps us to recognize that God cannot be limited to any ONE image (see above), and it helps us to see something more of the reflection of the whole of humanity in its Creator. If a girl grows up seeing only men and boys in the sanctuary, singing hymns that refer to "men", "brotherhood" and "sons" far more than they ever refer even to the whole of humanity, let alone the other half, and hearing and reading only male images of God, she can be forgiven for thinking that God and the Church are not very interested in her or her gender. Yet there were women and girls in whom Jesus was interested, quite against the customs of his day. The Samaritan woman at the well (John 4:5–29) Jairus's daughter, and the woman with a haemorrhage, (Luke 8:40–56), Mary Magdalene, Joanna and Susanna and "many other women" (Luke 8:2 and 3) were treated by Jesus in a revolutionary way, which evidently endeared them to him, in that they were the ones who remained with him to the end.

Why has the Church told women otherwise, for all these years?

Take the stories of Jairus's daughter and the woman who touched Jesus's clothes. They were two nameless females brought to healing and new life by Jesus. One was only a child, the daughter of a society leader. Their social settings were quite different. Although it was quite in order for Jairus, a man, to approach Jesus, he did risk pollution in the dense crowd in his fatherly concern. He was a public person who requested private treatment for his family. Yet in the midst of that crowd was another person, a woman, whose desperation brought her out of her private cultural rejection into public scrutiny. She had no right to approach Jesus, but was drawn to him.

On the one hand we have the rich, privileged male using his cultural rights to secure healing – on the other the penniless (she had spent all her money on doctors) isolated female, relying solely upon the still small voice of faith within her in the hope of a return to her, albeit limited, life.

The child had apparently died, but her father's faith in Jesus was not discouraged. The woman had all but died to her family and local community (see the Old Testament book of Leviticus where blood is a separating, unclean thing), but her faith hadn't been squashed by the hostile religious system. Notice how Jesus perceived the touch he wasn't supposed to feel, though his disciples hadn't even noticed the woman, and how Jesus heard the message of Jairus's daughter's death which he wasn't meant to hear.

He urged faith – and there were miracles all round! The daughter and the woman were two who, in the order of things in Israel at that time, were very much second-class citizens, yet Jesus concentrated his attention on each of them, and saw right to the heart of the problem.

Pictures of dying children come frequently into our lives on T V and hoardings to tear at our heart-strings, and usually our purse-strings too. But bleeding women are avoided by polite society – hushed tones confide, "It's women's problems", and no more is said. There are still today, in this country, Christian congregations, for instance the Greek Orthodox, where menstruating women are not allowed to receive communion. A perfectly natural function is regarded as unclean. This comes, presumably, from the Old Testament ideas of uncleanness, which, it seems to me, were formulated by pre-scientific men mystified by a peculiar phenomenon they couldn't explain. Sometimes when we're unsure, or frightened about things, we block them out or laugh at them, rather than learning to understand them.

In his relationship with these two females, Jesus affirmed God's creation of woman – a wonderful system, brilliantly rhymed and beautifully formed. And he takes womanhood by the hand so that we can stand up and be proud to claim our place in God's Kingdom.

Four
April – Easter

Living and working in a London borough which has a high proportion of elderly people has meant that my ministry has always included plenty of funeral services. We have four cemeteries in Newham, and several firms of undertakers always on the lookout for someone to take a "nice" service.

"Nice" in this case means that I have to be willing to contact the bereaved family before the funeral, so that I can make note of any special features of the deceased, not least the name by which (s)he was known. You would be amazed at the number of people, particularly those born before World War II, who aren't known by their first Christian name, or use a completely different name, picked up somewhere along the line ("Sonny" or "Lally", for example). I found it very important to try to read between the lines – it wasn't so much what they told me about their loved one as how they said it. Sometimes I'd get the feeling that to say that, for example, a wife was "at last reunited" with her husband, might not be the great joy that one would wish! It was also very helpful to get some idea of who would be at the funeral – and whether or not they were speaking to each other. Once, while I was waiting for a funeral to arrive, a lady asked me, rather aggressively, whose "right" it was to sit in

the front row of the chapel. It appeared that her
father had been married twice, so there were two
separate families. It was with great relief that I
realized that this particular chapel had two front
rows, either side of the aisle, so civil war was not
declared.

On another occasion, I was asked if I would say
a short funeral service with a woman at the Chapel
of Rest, as, since she was not speaking to her
brother, she wouldn't attend her mother's funeral
service at the crematorium. I wasn't sure how I felt
about that. Would it just increase the anger and
encourage the rift, which, since the woman lived
abroad, would probably be irrevocably widened
when it was all over? Was I in a position to help
heal the hurts between them? If I refused to do the
short service at the undertaker's, would she be
persuaded to come to the family's service? I felt that
that wasn't really helpful, and might just make
things worse, so I duly attended the undertaker's
chapel and tried to help this woman come to terms
with the guilt she felt about moving so far away
from her mother that she'd not been able to help
with her care. At the same time we prayed for
reconciliation between brother and sister. At the end
of the service, the woman suddenly said that she
now had the courage to face her brother and ask
his forgiveness, and see if they could make peace.
I could do no more than commend them to God
and wait.

It was with great joy and thanksgiving, as well
as damp eyes and misted-over glasses that I saw the
brother and sister walk hand-in-hand into the chapel
next day. Truly a resurrection in the face of death

– and I'm sure that God, and their mother, smiled too.

Sometimes it's very difficult to speak to anyone before the funeral. The family of the one who has died may live very far away, and not have a telephone. In those cases, I always ask the undertakers to show the mourners to their seats so that I can introduce myself and have a quick chat with them before the coffin is brought in – by which time, of course, the poor bearers are wilting under the weight. But, even so, it's just so hard to conduct a service which is at all relevant if I know nothing at all about the person who has died, and those surrounding them.

I was once asked to conduct the funeral of a man who had died in his early forties. He was single, and his brother had made the funeral arrangements but was not on the telephone. When the cortège arrived, I watched the family get out of the cars and two men, I have to say somewhat tough looking, got out with an elderly lady between them. "That's the deceased's mother," whispered the undertaker, "she's blind." I moved forward, ready to shake hands, hoping thus to make some contact with her. The man to her left pushed me out of the way. "She's blind," he said. "Can't see you!", and carried on into the chapel. I hurried in behind them, very anxious to find out my all-important details.

"What name was your brother known by?" I asked.

"Ted," said one brother. "Eddie," said the other, firmly.

"Right," I said. "Now he was only young, wasn't he; did he die suddenly?"

"It was the drink," said one brother.

"You can't say that," said the other, "just say he was ill."

"Well, em, what sort of work did he do then?"

"He didn't."

"I see. How would you describe him? What sort of fellow was he?" I asked desperately.

"A layabout."

"I see, em, but friendly, was he? Sociable?"

"He'd drink with anybody," said the brother, and it was clear from the faces in the chapel that everybody had been drinking in his memory.

So with those few, telling details about my subject, I started the service, carefully alternating the name by which I called him so that no one would be upset.

I usually invite the congregation to read the 23rd Psalm with me during the service, but I was in two minds with this particular congregation, who seemed aggressive, disinterested and drunk. But I took courage and invited them as usual, and have never heard the Psalm read with such gusto. Perhaps the booze had removed the inhibitions people sometimes feel in a church situation, but whatever it was the service came alive for us all then, and everybody seemed very happy when it was over, no doubt ready to continue their drinking.

All the undertakers with whom I've worked have been hardworking and usually very cheerful, and they all have the rather disconcerting ability to say the most outrageous things under their breath, with a completely straight face, which has me struggling for composure at just the wrong moment. To the undertakers, a "nice" service is a relatively short one, as they are always off to do another, or at least some of their cars and drivers will be needed by another firm. Most undertakers are very good at sizing up their clients, and know instinctively what sort of a "do" this will be. Often, they know the family if they are local — families around here tend to use "their" undertaker through the generations, and although there are huge conglomerates, we have also some smaller family firms who have served their neighbourhoods for years.

There are quite distinct different strands of tradition. There is the typical East-End family, who will have "the horses" (a horse-drawn hearse), masses of elaborate floral tributes, and who will be dressed entirely in very glamorous black. That funeral would usually culminate in a burial, though with land getting scarcer and more expensive, burials are not as frequent as they used to be.

Then there is the rather plainer family, who have a very straightforward funeral, with lots of cellophane-covered sheaves of flowers and the standard hearse and limousines. There's also the radical family who arrive in their own cars carrying bunches of garden flowers and who ask to read some poetry.

I have often wondered about the whole business of funeral flowers, which sometimes are worth literally thousands of pounds at one funeral. Florists are most inventive and will attempt to make almost anything out of flowers for a funeral tribute. I have seen teddy bears, a docker's hook, a billiard table, a cup of tea, a bingo card (4' x 3') with Gran's numbers picked out in flowers, a telephone, and a pack of "Rizla" papers (with which you "roll your own" cigarettes).

I always thought these lavish displays a terrible waste – and indeed I think I still do believe it of the elaborate shapes – and I told the undertakers to buy my flowers now, when I can enjoy them. But once I was asked to conduct a funeral for the stillborn daughter of a young African couple. I met the mother in hospital, who told me that she would not come to the funeral, as in their tradition, women don't go to funerals. So the next day I was confronted by four young African men who joined in the short service very reverently. As usual, I asked the baby's father if he would like to carry his daughter's coffin to the grave, which he did, while his friends followed behind. As we walked, the friends pulled leaves and small branches from trees lining the path, and when the coffin was put into the grave, they threw the leaves and branches down too. It made me think that perhaps our modern floral tributes are a throwback to an ancient idea – maybe it says something about the waste of life. I have now revised my funeral instructions, and have asked that there should be some beautiful fresh flowers on the coffin and in the church – but please no large spectacles made of carnations!

So much of the business of death is taken care of on our behalf by other agencies these days. Most people die in hospital, from where they are collected by undertakers, laid out, embalmed and dressed ready to be (sometimes) viewed by their relatives. I have often been asked whether it is "right" to see the body of a loved one at the funeral parlour (or "Chapel of Rest"), and I always feel that, if there is doubt, then the person should go. I say this because unless they are quite sure that they don't want to see their loved one's body, there's always a possibility that later they will wish they had. My dear friend Elaine couldn't bear to see the body of her stillborn son, but later felt that she'd let him down by not doing so. People have sometimes said their goodbyes in hospital, but long to see their loved one relaxed and out of pain. Sometimes, when a person has died suddenly and unexpectedly there's a need to say goodbye properly, and maybe also to say other things that were not said before. When another friend's husband died while he was abroad, it was very important for her to see his body before she could begin to believe that he was dead.

In the not so distant past, most people died at home, and were laid out by their family, and perhaps a person in the neighbourhood who specialized in such things. Then they would lie in state in the front room for a few days until the funeral. In nine years' ministry, I have known the body to be "brought home" in about a dozen cases, and I have been asked to go to say prayers over the body with the family. If you can bear it, I think it's a lovely thing to do.

But, I think I might find it hard to let my loved one go again, when the day came for the funeral. It's a difficult, terribly emotional day, but absolutely essential for the grieving process to proceed. At the funeral, last goodbyes are said and the parting is made quite final, perhaps more vividly at a burial than at a cremation. Some West Indian families fill in the grave themselves, but most families throw a token handful of earth on to the coffin and leave the filling-in to the gravediggers – who these days

51

often use a JCB. But I found it terribly hard to put even one shovel of earth on my friend Jen Joy's grave — so much for my recomendations of "primitive ritual".

The funeral usually starts the real business of grieving. Up until then, there's so much to do, and the family are numb with shock, anyway. But at the funeral, the grim reality begins to dawn, and it's the acceptance of the reality that is the beginning of healing. It's a long, lonely, difficult business, grief, and people generally say that it will be around two years before it is truly over. Then, of course, one doesn't continue life as before, but rather learns to accept that particular gap and live with it.

People have often wondered how I could cope with being so near to so much death and grief, but I always tell them that through my funeral ministry I have heard so many real love-stories — stories of loyalty and patience, where a daughter or son or partner has cared for their loved one day in, day out, for years and years — far beyond what might be called "duty" or even personal capacity. And that keeping on keeping on is real love in action; a glimpse of God's love and, indeed, many people would say that they have gained unexpected strength from God when they really thought that they'd come to the end of their tether.

And the incredible thing is that that love isn't wasted. Somehow it is held up to God as an offering and it is recognized and cherished by the God who watched Jesus die; the God who every day sees beloved children starving to death or killing each other; the God who goes on loving even on the cross, giving us the perfect example of longsuffering. It's not at all dramatic. It's painful and exhausting to keep on loving but that is what Jesus told us to do.

And we keep on loving, even when someone has died; perhaps we are relieved and pleased for them to be out of their sufferings, but we miss them and need to go on talking about them, laughing as well as crying when we remember them. That way the love goes on, reflecting a relationship that has affected our lives.

Jesus's friends were ordinary people like us, who were so touched by his love that they were changed; but it was his death and resurrection that made the difference to all humanity, when he showed that death was not the end, but the beginning of something better.

Nothing can take away the excruciating pain at the death of someone we love, but if we can believe that they are safe with God in Heaven, and that one day we may meet again, we affirm the eternal thread of love that binds us to each other and, ultimately, to God.

Five

May

"Consider the Lilies . . ."

As I was over the age of thirty, had three children and several part-time jobs when I wanted to be trained for ordination, I was allowed to join the Gilmore course – sadly no longer in existence – which operated from Queen's College, Birmingham. It was a non-residential course where we had to attend college for one week in each term to hear lectures and see our tutors in order to collect the assignments which we had to complete by the next time we went to college. We were linked to a person living near us, perhaps a recently ordained deacon, who helped us week by week, and guided our studies. It was an excellent course, and I loved my weeks in Birmingham playing at being a student. The best part was that we were able to mix with others in similar situations to ourselves, juggling kids, jobs and essays, and give each other encouragement and support. But the topic which absorbed more of our conversation than any other was, without doubt, the all-important issue of "What are we going to wear when we are ordained?"

I do know that Jesus exhorted us, his followers, not to worry what we would wear each day; that God would provide clothing for us, just as God did for the lilies – but the lilies wear the same thing all the time. And lilies aren't women deacons, in the public eye.

When I was first made deaconess, we had to wear a navy blue cassock, which is a sort of high-necked, full-length, coat-type garment, with a heavy silver cross. Some of the other students felt that they would have an amended design which would be normal coat length – but wouldn't that look odd in church if we had to wear a white surplice over it? Some felt that a plain navy dress, rather like a nun wears, was sufficient, but I guess that those were the ones whose churches were modern buildings which were well-heated. We all certainly wanted our uniform to be flattering to our feminine form – though people's interpretations of that differed, depending on whether they wanted their figures exphasized or enveloped.

I had something of a dilemma, in that my work took me from the special care baby unit, in the maternity hospital, which is kept at sub-tropical temperatures, via the educated pre-fab, at St James's, which, though starting cool, quickly warmed up, to St John's, the Victorian barn in the middle of the High Street, which was icy on all but the hottest days of summer. The answer was conjured up by my friend Doris, who made a woollen cassock, gently fitted, but with sufficient room underneath it to wear a couple of jumpers and thick trousers and boots if necessary. I wore this outfit very successfully for seven years, the only problem being that, deaconesses being rather thin on the ground, no one quite knew what it meant, except that it was something holy. When it came to my ordination as a deacon, when I had to change my navy cassock

for a black one, with space for a clerical collar, Doris
kept to the same pattern, with the added refinement
of a pink satin lining which, of course, does not
show, but makes me feel nicer.

At least the collar is instantly recognizable as
something religious, but I like always to wear the
WHOLE outfit – cassock and collar – OR just
ordinary clothes. Some of my friends have pretty
flowery blouses and dresses with tunnels for their
clerical collar, but I think that that looks as
incongruous as the men do when they wear jeans,
sweatshirts and brightly coloured shirts with a
clerical collar too.

I normally wear "the full gear" when I'm doing
specifically church work – conducting services,
visiting in hospital or at home – and I find it useful
in that (a) it saves me having to decide what to wear:
(b) it seems to give me almost automatic entry into
almost anywhere; and (c) as I put it on I assume my
"confident" face. It is indeed a valuable garment.

Though it has its drawbacks, of course, in that,
if I wear it all day, I sometimes put on anything at
all underneath or even, if it's hot, not very much.
This means that I cannot take it off in public, so am
obliged to go shopping, or collect the children from
school, or go the the bank, in full uniform. The
problem with that being that I CANNOT be
inconspicuous thus attired, and people in shops or
bank queues feel quite at liberty to ask all sorts of
questions – most of which I am unable to answer.
Questions such as, "Did Eve have sex with her sons?"
and, "Why did the clergyman who conducted my
mother's funeral have dirty fingernails?" I am also,
especially if there has recently been anything on

television on the subject, required to give a quick run-down on the pros and cons of women's ordination. I must say, though, that that is usually a great opportunity and I try to rise to it, as often I am the first woman that people have encountered so dressed – especially in Marks and Spencer's.

I remember once, just after Christmas, conducting a funeral for a rather "posh" couple whose aunt had died. They were the only mourners, and thanked me warmly for the service, which they had much appreciated. Before my next funeral, I dashed home, as my son Dominic, then aged six, was very keen to spend his Christmas money at the earliest opportunity – as, of course, was every other child in Newham, and so the store was packed. Having bought his toy, Dominic wanted to sit on the floor and get it out of the box. But I did not have much time and so, with some agitation, I eventually dragged Dominic out of the store, both of us yelling – to look straight at the "posh" couple whose car was caught in the traffic outside the shop!

I suppose that most of us have a "work" persona, which is exaggerated if we have to wear a uniform. Clergy, of all people perhaps, feel constrained to behave in a particular manner, as many people expect us to behave in a certain way. Thus I am allowed immediately into people's homes, managers' offices, the inner enclaves of hospital premises, and all sorts of other places – I guess because people assume that I will be harmless – or that I have some official function (I did say that my uniform makes me feel more confident in myself).

But it also has its converse side, as people express surprise if I am at all interested in worldly things.

One lady, when I mentioned money to her, said that she thought I shouldn't be interested in such a corrupt subject. I pointed out that, even in uniform, I am still expected to pay for goods in shops.

Some people are surprised that I am a sexual being, and find the modern trappings of fashion – nail varnish, make-up, coloured tights – inappropriate for me, even when I'm not in uniform. The fact that I am twice-married with three children, is difficult for some others to accept, as, of course, is the fact that my language tends to reflect my East-End schooling, and my life's experience!

Just before I was married, I saw a friend who is a community nurse, and asked her some questions about contraception. She talked for a while, but then suddenly said, "I can't cope with talking about sex to someone in a cassock and clerical collar"!

I have thought a great deal about this, and I think that her comment says something very important about people's attitude to the Church, and also about women's ordination. I feel that some people do not like to mix their sexuality with their spirituality. They like to approach God having left aside their everyday selves, which includes their sexual selves. In church they don't want to be reminded of their sexual desires – hence perhaps the Bishop of London's declaration that if he saw a woman in the pulpit he would want to put his arm around her – and that's why he doesn't feel that it's right that women should be taking leading roles at church. It makes me wonder if, perhaps, the Bishop doesn't realize that women in the pews have been lusting after the men in the sanctuary for centuries. I know that some men find it hard to credit women with sexual desire – but they're wrong. The fact is, that God has created humans with sexual desire for each other, and, if used and not abused, the satisfaction of that desire creates not only the next generation, but also a move towards wholeness in humans. When he found out that Christopher and I were to be married, our dear friend, Alan Webster, erstwhile Dean of St Paul's Cathedral, wrote to us that, in our love for each other, "you will find out so much more about yourselves, each other and God".

If we leave our sexual selves outside church, we do not bring our whole selves into our relationship with God, and that's sad. God gave us these desires to enjoy – though they are often the cause of great unhappiness – and our sexuality should be as much an offering of ourselves as any other aspect of our being. The Church has to take a lot of the responsibilities for making people feel that their sexual selves are wrong and sinful – for so long, the Church has concentrated on saying, "Thou shalt not" rather than "Thou shalt", and so the Church (us) must work hard at redressing the balance by lifting the guilt and encouraging positive feelings about sexuality. By introducing a true balance of humanity into the priesthood, for example, we could say that ALL of humanity is equally capable of representing us to God and God to us. I do think, too, that this would be faithful to Jesus's attitude to women, which was, though scantily reported in the gospels, quite revolutionary. Jesus was happy to allow women near him (Luke 8:2, 3), and encouraged a woman called Mary to listen to theological discussions (Luke 10:42).

But Jesus's equal opportunities policy has sadly

been neglected by his followers these last two thousand years. Social conditions have made it difficult, I admit, but at last moves have now been made towards the sort of equality that Jesus seems to have expected.

People might say that it is precisely BECAUSE we women at college talked incessantly of what we might wear that we should not be made priests. They might think, perhaps, that women would worry more about such practicalities, and not be fully involved with their work. But I feel that having their feet firmly grounded in issues of warmth, comfort and sustenance actually enables women's theology to spring from real life, where people ARE, rather than several feet above their heads and beyond their understanding.

The other day a lady asked me if I knew another woman deacon called Sylvia. "She comes here to preach sometimes," said the lady, "or should I say TALK rather than preach." I suggested that perhaps what the lady meant was that she could actually understand what Sylvia said. "Yes, that's it," she said. "Sylvia talks about everyday things, things that I know about. It MEANS something to me when Sylvia preaches. Sometimes when the men preach I come out of church not having understood a word."

For me, that conversation said it all. The lady felt that that was what theology was all about – something that SHE couldn't understand, but that educated MEN were privy to. It seems to me that Jesus said quite the opposite; he said that the meek, the poor, the lowly and unlovely inherit the earth, and that faith in God is not about what we KNOW intellectually, but what we FEEL in our hearts. And

I think that there's something about women and the way that God has made us, that makes it possible for us to communicate that to people easily and naturally. And what better qualification for priesthood?

Six
June – Father's Day

When you pray, say "Our Father".

As my father never tires of reminding me, I made a very good choice of parents, and throughout my life he has certainly proved that my "choice" was right.

My father was the youngest child of my grandfather's second wife's five children, his first wife having died in the birth of her first child. My grandfather insisted that this child was to be named after him – Harry. No frills, no Harold or Henry, no middle name, just Harry. Sadly, my father never really knew his father very well, as Harry Senior became ill with tuberculosis when my father was six, and got steadily worse until he died four years later.

As the child of what would nowadays be called a single-parent family, my father had no shortage of authority figures, as he lived in a close-knit community on the Isle of Dogs, in East London, surrounded by relatives. His older sister's husbands and his brothers became father substitutes, and, just after starting work in the Graving Dock at fourteen, the Second World War began. The East End suffered very heavy bombing, and one night, while he was fire-watching, someone shouted that his home had suffered a direct hit and was on fire. He dashed home, to find his mother and sisters rescuing things from the inferno, and he's always been puzzled by the fact that, instead of rescuing useful or valuable things, they brought out a curious mixture of odds and ends. My grandfather had played football professionally for Millwall, and had won cups and medals, but they were left and never seen again. Instead, the everyday cutlery was rescued (in a pillow-case) and, although it was summer, my aunt's very precious fur coat. The family then walked the ten miles or so to Dagenham, where the eldest sister lived, and where they later set up home, and whence my father left to join the Merchant Navy.

It's a favourite after-dinner game of mine to ask people what, assuming that all the people and pets are out of *their* blazing home, they would want to save most. It's fascinating to hear what people regard as irreplaceable, and it often stimulates interesting discussions on the value of things in our lives.

I suppose that my father's family, like most of us, had never thought that such a tragedy would happen, and therefore hadn't prepared.

But are we EVER prepared for the shocks that puncture our lives? A man was telling me how, in the early 80s, he and his wife often marvelled at their modest success and their secure happiness as a family. Although people around them had traumas and difficulties they seemed to have escaped. Until, that is, late in 1982, when their lives were shattered by one drama after another.

The wife's father died suddenly; the husband's almost assured promotion was dashed from him, which meant that the house they had bought in anticipation of the new job became cripplingly expensive; the wife lost her job in a merger; their son was badly injured in an accident at school; and their dog was run over and killed. They got to a point where they dreaded the telephone ringing for fear of what else could happen to them. The man told me how vulnerable they felt, and how futile and fragile their former security then seemed.

Thanks to their faith in God and each other, and some good friends to support them, that family recovered and continued to grow – severely chastened and vowing never to feel too secure again.

In order to grow, we must, to a certain extent, feel secure, but at the same time aware of the constantly changing nature of life. Even the most desired changes involve loss. Take, for example, the advent of the longed-for baby – no matter how lovely she is, there are losses of freedom, and changed roles which mean that lives are irrevocably altered, and it is a changed family unit that moves on. My sister Suzanne put it very clearly when she said that, while she was pregnant, everyone asked how SHE was, but after she'd had Gregory, she was hardly given a sideways glance, as people wanted to know how HE was. Such is motherhood.

Jesus said that we must not put our faith in money and property, but look for God's Kingdom first (Matthew 6:33). When we begin to feel secure in God's love and thus ourselves, we can bear to risk a little.

But, of course, risks and opportunities do not always present themselves when we feel at our best and most secure, and, just like my father's family, we sometimes behave strangely or irrationally when a shock throws us off balance. Jesus said that we must ALWAYS be ready – "Watch therefore, for you do not know on what day your Lord is coming". The next door that opens for us may be the trap-door through which the bottom of our world will fall, and the only real preparation for any change, good or bad, is faith. The sort of faith that practises risk, growth and change in good times will be the faith that, in bad times, even the end of the world, lets us fall into God's arms.

And in God's arms is just where my father wished that he was, no doubt, when travelling the high seas in a merchant ship during World War II.

My father always says that, when they were being given the little training that was available, the emphasis was very much on shooting the enemy, with no warning of the fact that the enemy would be trying to shoot them. But, banded together with other young men on this little tub in the middle of the ocean, I imagine that fear was something that they did their best to ignore. There was lots else to do, not least to get to know each other, and it was really my father's first venture out of his home area, where everybody was of very similar class and background. At sea, he mixed with men from other parts of the country and from other backgrounds, where public school and assured jobs were all part of the picture. My father's eyes were opened to ideas which had never occurred to him at home, and though frightening, his time at sea was an education broader than any he'd known before.

My father met my mother at a dance hall (long since turned into a warehouse), and before long they were corresponding regularly, and they married, like thousands more couples, as soon as the war was over, in 1945. My mother had always wanted four sons, but instead was blessed with two daughters, but it was not really until Mother resumed her work as a book-keeper that my father took a more active part in our lives.

My parents each worked outside the home part-time, but my father's work continued at his desk at home, which thereby allowed him much more flexibility than most fathers have. It was my father who taught us how to make scones and how to play cricket, using a bat that he'd made. When my aunt was coming home from Australia, and new cushion covers were needed to brighten up the sitting-room for the party, it was my father who ironed the embroidery transfer (a free gift from a magazine) onto four pieces of red material, so that we could each sew a robin sitting on a branch. We were quite used to seeing my father cook, clean, sew, hang out washing, as well as mend the car and fit new window-frames. My mother's multiple sclerosis was diagnosed in 1961, and since then my father has spent more and more time caring for her, as she is now almost completely paralysed.

Always a political animal, my father enjoys a lively debate about all sorts of issues, and often puts his comments in letters to the BBC, several of which have been read out. He enjoys music of all sorts, and has a warm sense of humour – not always easy in his circumstances. My father often argues with me about things – he was very sad when I gave up further education to become a nurse, but he never made me feel that I must do it to prove him wrong. He has always supported my sister and me in whatever we wanted to do, and is a keen critic of my work. I can rely on him and my mother to tell me the truth about my performance, at church or on TV or radio.

With such a lovely experience of being fathered, I have no difficulty with thinking of God as Father. The warm and supporting love, the generous and encouraging interest, the occasional spoiling, that I have enjoyed in my earthly father I can easily transfer to my experiences of a heavenly Father. The God who is tender and loving, yet allows his children to make their own mistakes and still welcomes them with open arms, is pictured so clearly in the Bible; and I can understand people who feel that, being such a good motif, it should remain the only one for all time.

The Bible is an extremely patriarchal book, and it is interesting that Jesus's genealogy is traced back in Matthew's gospel via his father, Joseph, since one has always been a Jew if one's mother were a Jew (she being the only parent of whom one can be certain). The importance of "fathering nations" is very much to the fore in the Old Testament, with its implications not just biologically, but in terms of leadership and decision-making too. In the New Testament, Joseph's visit by an angel and his acceptance of the news (Matthew 1:18–25) are rather overshadowed by Mary's visit and acceptance. But although not a central figure in many people's idea of the Nativity of Jesus, the course of history would have been changed if Joseph had not agreed to do as the Angel of the Lord told him. Our Lord's birth and childhood must have been strongly affected by Joseph's presence, for without him, the family would have been in a sorry state.

Joseph seems to have been the strong, silent type

of man, whom some might brand "boring", yet I think that he was perhaps one of those very important people who are utterly reliable, who keep on keeping on in the face of great difficulty and also when it's routine and dull. Their sort of love is probably not terribly inspired or romantically imaginative, they aren't given to magical phraseology (St Joseph never speaks in the gospels), and they wouldn't dream of doing anything on the spur of the moment. They carry on loving when they don't feel like it – when the beloved is being an absolute pain, in the middle of the night, or when they'd rather be doing something else.

My friend Ken was an only child who left home to join the Army, but in time his father died and his mother became ill. By then his mother lived in smaller accommodation where there was no room for him, so, living a couple of miles away, Ken would make the journey to his mother's home every morning, wash and dress her, and give her breakfast. Every evening, after work, except every other Tuesday, when a cousin helped out, he would go to his mother's, cook her a meal and get her ready for bed. He did that every single day for more than ten years, until his mother died. Like many, many other carers, Ken laid down his life for his mother, but without dying, and that actually requires a very special sort of long-suffering love that Jesus means us to have for one another.

It seems that Jesus learnt the example of that sort of love from his father, who made a conscious decision, not out of guilt, nor out of a self-satisfied sense of martyrdom, to give generously of himself for the benefit of others, and in obedience to God's command. That decision couldn't have been taken lightly, or in a moment of mad passion – neither could it come from one who had no experience of being loved himself; "keeping on loving" is exhausting and not often satisfying in itself, for so often the object of the love becomes more ill and less able, and therefore one needs support and encouragement in it.

There will always be some people who love the limelight, and need to be in the grip of passion at all times; these are the ones who do extraordinary, sometimes wonderful, things that make the headlines. There are a lot of us in the middle range – we occasionally break out, but more often keep to routine. But then there are the Josephs of this world, who make a quiet decision and then keep to it, not saying much, through thick and thin. I knew a woman who was married during the last war. While her husband was abroad he met another woman and decided to stay with her, and asked his wife to release him from their marriage. She said that he could do as he pleased, but that she had vowed to remain married to him until death, and so she lived alone for the next fifty years, because to her that was the right thing to do.

Perhaps it was from his dear father that Jesus learnt of God as father, and was able to pass that on to his followers. He knew that ultimately, nothing, not even family, must get in the way of our relationship with God, yet I'm sure Jesus also knew that God's love is often brought to us in other people, and it is through them that we learn about God.

So that when God gave us fathers, he gave us, at best, an idea of God's self. God gave us an idea of a loving and protecting parent on whom we depend heavily at first for the practicalities of life, but from whom, in time, we must gradually break away, to grow into a different, no less respectful, but more mature, relationship. Perhaps it is a slightly more romatic relationship than that which we have with our mothers, who, having fed us and changed our nappies, have a more down-to-earth idea of our shortcomings. Fathers, often avoiding the more basic duties of parenthood, can have a vision for us, untrammelled by our digestive problems, or whatever.

I know that some people, more it seems these days, do not even know their fathers, which is to me especially sad. We need the creative tension of a relationship to bring us towards wholeness, and I think that that's why God created humans the way we are, needing two people to get us going. For those who are less fortunate, may I suggest adopting St Joseph, who doesn't say much, but is always there, keeping an eye on us from Heaven.

Seven
July – Celebrate the Children

Jesus said, "Let the children come to me".

At the height of the summer, the evenings are long and our windows are open, and there seem to be children everywhere – running, shouting to each other, sitting on walls chewing gum. Exams over, the schools diversify, and sports days and swimming galas, open evenings and dramatic productions take over from schoolwork. Yet another batch of hopefuls is released from the school system into the job market, and, while good bets are snapped up, the not-so-fortunate hang around at the bottom of the pile and try yet another training scheme.

Anyone who has had children enjoys the schooldays but dreads them ending, and waits with bated breath until the child is settled on a path that looks towards job satisfaction and security one way or another.

I was really sad when my schooldays were over, and it seemed a very harsh and cold world as I looked around. I'd been to a lovely secondary school – a co-educational grammar six or seven miles further into East London, which lived in a magnificent old building with a hall modelled on the hold of a tea-clipper ship. The school's founder, George Green, had generously devoted some of his money and time to give some poor children from the East End (boys only at first) an education; and, by the time I got to it, the school had an excellent reputation, and attracted children from quite a wide area.

It was only a small school with two hundred or so pupils and a staff of about fifteen. Teachers and rooms often did double duty – the biology master taking a class swimming for instance, and a classroom being used for children to eat their packed lunches in.

It was while sitting on a desk in just such a room that one of the "big boys" twirled his duffle bag around his head with such vigour that the string broke and the bag hurtled towards my face and smashed my glasses. Sadly, I was unable to persuade the head that my wounds were serious enough to be taken to hospital in the P.E. master's sports car (shame), so the drama was soon over. That is, until about twenty-five years later, when I looked up from the opening prayer at a funeral to see the bag's owner sitting in the congregation. As they filed out at the end, I couldn't resist reminding him that he was the one who'd broken my glasses, and he told me that he'd been wondering all through the service whether I would remember him!

With such a small school, it was possible for the head to know almost all his pupils and their families, a relationship which was deepened when every year he accompanied a group on a school holiday abroad – one year to a French-speaking country, the next to a German-speaking one – and always amazed us with the extent of his knowledge of the world.

On one trip to Austria, the dancing teacher accompanied us, and insisted that four of the girls should perform a sword dance (which she was teaching us in school at the time) as a gesture of thanks for the hospitality extended to us in one rather unsuspecting Austrian village. So that evening found three friends and me, all London's East-Enders to the bone, doing Scottish sword dances in a floodlit Austrian castle courtyard. Our hosts seemed delighted and we were very proud of ourselves, but looking back it all seems quite bizarre.

There were drawbacks in going to such a small school, of course – the beautiful hall was not only assembly room, examination hall, library and gym, but dinner hall as well, with all the tables and equipment having to be laboriously stacked away between each session. Also, there was a limit to the subjects which could be studied, but certainly no shortage of enthusiasm on the part of the teachers, who could impart information to people who, for the most part, anyway, seemed quite keen to learn and get on.

The school's founder had been a devout Congregationalist, and the school was firmly grounded in Christian principles and teaching. There was heavy emphasis on service towards others in the school, and to the local community. Almost everyone belonged to a club or group, and as a raw first-former I was taught to play chess by the then head boy, who seemed to me terribly grown up – almost a MAN. We also collected money each week for various good causes, and when my sister was in charge of the "Goodwill Scheme" she had the whole school knitting squares to make into blankets. So although perhaps we didn't have the widest academic opportunities, we certainly had a real all-round education in the broadest sense of the word.

Alan Bennett said, "Education is what you remember when you forget all that you've been taught", and certainly, most of what we learn in school lessons is pretty useless in everyday life. But it's what we pick up almost without noticing it that really matters. It's learning to live together in a group – the first group that we experience outside our family; it's learning to listen to and to respect someone whose views are different from our own; it's an interest being fanned into a passion by one who cares enough to have a vision that can make it happen; but most of all it's about wisdom – that quality which is only caught, never taught.

Above the main door to our school was the legend – "The fear of the Lord, that is wisdom; and to depart from evil is understanding" (Job 28:28) and, in a sense, to have that written at the entrance to a place where examinations and book learning were of great importance somehow doesn't quite add up. Yet what was important wasn't what was taught, but rather *how* it was taught. "Knowledge is power" proclaims the advertisement for a local radio news station, whose idea, of course, is to attract more listeners with the promise of being lifted out of a dreary, powerless life, with lots of newsy information. Actually, knowledge on its own is pretty powerless – the real knack is learning how and when to use it and that's wisdom.

Jesus told the story (Matthew 25:14–30; Luke 19:11–27) of a man who had to go away from home for a while. He gave each of three servants some of his money to look after, and the first immediately invested his share, as did the second, but the third was frightened and hid the money. When the master returned, he was delighted with the results of the investments but furious with the third man, saying that, if he'd only put the money in an ordinary bank at least he'd have a small amount of interest.

It seems terribly sad to us to think of the poor man, who thought he was doing his best, but didn't want to risk anything. There is a part of each of us that is afraid of venturing outside our known circle, and we can sympathize, especially when, as he says to his boss, "I know that you are a hard man".

Surely it is wisdom that encourages us to use our knowledge to step outside ourselves, and to move on to some new and exciting place in our lives. It is no use teaching children facts unless, at the same time, they absorb the confidence to use them.

Part of our reluctance to use our knowledge is a fear that we may lose something — status, power or the security of a known commodity, perhaps — but then all decisions involve the rejection of something. If we decide to do one thing, we are simultaneously deciding not to do something else. Sharing knowledge may mean that someone else has an opportunity to use it, even against us — like the countries which have acquired nuclear powered missiles — and that's a risk we have to take. Knowledge kept to ourselves makes no one any richer, and denies us the opportunity of seeing people and ideas grow and develop.

These days it's very important to have knowledge and to know how to use it, in order to make enough money to live on. For some people this becomes an all-consuming passion, on which they spend all their time and energy, leaving them with little space to enjoy the fruits of their labour — they have only the energy to tot up the interest, and watch the bank balance rise. John Wesley said that people decrease in grace as they increase in wealth, and we all know the bores who can only talk about how much they've got. But, in the end, money is worth no more than it can buy − it has no intrinsic value, and, as the Beatles sang, "Money can't buy me love".

Money is no comfort if we're lonely. We can't talk to it or give it a cuddle, neither will it listen to us or cuddle us back. Yes, we need it, and, with the gulf between rich and poor becoming ever greater, I could suggest many people whose lives would change from miserable to almost bearable with the acquisition of a largish sum of money. It is quite right and just that all people should have a warm, secure home, with enough to eat, and cash to spare for whatever their fancy takes. It is not right or just that a few should be spending huge amounts on inflated luxuries, while many lie awake at night worrying whether their home will be repossessed, or their gas bill prove unpayable, or worse, that a child should want to go on a school trip, or even need its tonsils removed.

Wisdom is about understanding how to use knowledge so that the world is a better place; so that the power which comes with knowledge is put to the good of many people. John Wesley − who came from a well-to-do family and had quite a lot to say about money − said, "Money never stays with me − I throw it out of my hands in case it should find its way into my heart", and he obviously understood the temptation to accumulate, as if money were sufficient in itself. He also said, "Make all you can; save all you can; give all you can", and if we can teach our children to share ALL the good things that are on offer in this world, we ensure their future.

Jesus was ready to give time to children, Matthew (19:13–15), Mark (10:13–16) and Luke (18:15–17) all record an attempt by some people to bring their children to Jesus. They wanted him to touch the children, who were not only very precious in themselves, but especially so to people who live on the land, who need all the labourers they can get, and they were always important to the Jews as the continuation of the race. The disciples shooed the people away, perhaps feeling that childen, being the noisy and not-always-controllable little darlings that they are, would bother Jesus, and get in the way. Perhaps they thought that Jesus should be concerned with more important issues – there is no record of the children being ill, for instance – and that the children would take time needed for other things. Perhaps the disciples were a bit jealous of the people and theirchildren; if they had any children themselves, they'd been left at home so that the men were free to be with Jesus; or maybe they had given up the possibility of having children in order to follow the Lord. Thus, people who wanted a fuss made of their children would remind the disciples of their lack of children, and we all know the thought that says, "Well if I've given it up, why can't they?"

But Jesus had different ideas. He was "angry" (Good News Bible), "indignant" (Revised Standard Version), quite an unusual emotion for Jesus, and he actually instructed the disciples to change their behaviour and make way for the children. He saw that the grown-ups had something to learn from the children, and reminded them that to receive the

Kingdom they must be "like a child".

Perhaps one of the most obvious characteristics of children is their simplicity; they are usually without guile, and take things at face value. Children are trusting creatures who normally will respond favourably to anyone who appears kind. Sadly, through the ages, people have capitalized on this, and have exerted their will over children in evil ways which somehow seem to make a pathetic adult feel momentarily powerful. So often these people are those whose own childhood was sad and loveless, and they are unable to change the pattern, afraid, as they are, ever to allow another adult to come close to them, for fear of being violated again, and the awful feeling of powerlessness and hopelessness which goes with it. These people have been robbed of their childhood, of the right of every human being to explore life and the world without care or prejudice, and to absorb a sense of one's own worth.

These days we have to warn our children against talking to strangers, but we thus prevent much harmless contact which gives joy not only to the children, but also to the adults who are touched by their unspoilt charm.

I've always tried to share my children a bit – partly to relieve the burden of single parenthood, but partly so that the children could learn about the world, and partly so that folk who for various reasons have no children of their own can enjoy the delicious sensation not only of sharing the children, but of giving them back! One of my lodgers always said that her time spent in our home, fun though it was, was better than any contraceptive, but, for me, having children was a most important element in my life, and the one which I most infrequently complain about. I don't think that I've been a very good mother (whatever she is) but I've certainly enjoyed being it, and have learnt, and go on learning, from the experience.

Maybe if we could see children as a corporate gift and responsibility, and a source from which we can ALL derive great pleasure – not to mention a future – then their voices drifting through our windows in the evenings, or even their presence at worship, would confirm the beauty and blessing of the whole of humanity – and remind us that once, we too were like that.

Eight
August
God rested from all his work which he had done

Although someone reminded me the other day that not everyone takes a holiday in August, with one of my children still at school the summer holidays have begun at the end of July each year for me for almost all my life. When I was at school six weeks seemed an eternity, stretching ahead, with sunshine every day and endless freedom and fun. Now that I am a parent, those six weeks seem hardly long enough to turn round in, still less to buy the essential new blazer and sports kit, which by the time I get round to it, will be available only in very small or extremely large sizes, or else be hideously expensive.

School holidays must directly affect perhaps half of the population in this country, and because of them August has quite a different feel from any other month. The rhythm of the days is different – no mums determinedly marching past in the mornings with children in tow; no lollipop lady, or trails of children, at the crossings; no traffic jams as they all go home again. A week in August is not so defined, because, without the children at school, every day is a Saturday.

For many people, school holidays are factory shutdowns too – but even if not, August is a time when families go away together, so that no school is missed. Of course, the holiday companies have capitalized on this fact, and the end of July and August are the most expensive times to take a break. I often think that June might be better for a holiday as the days are longer — but not so warm, of course, and anyway then there would be a long haul till Christmas, with only one August Bank holiday in between.

So, tradition dictates that tickets should be bought and cases packed; beach balls brought out of the back of the cupboard and examined, with airbeds, for punctures; last year's bucket and spade are produced unusable, by virtue of having been used for gardening; and none of the clothes currently in the wardrobe will be of any use at all because they were bought with Southend/Skye/Sardinia in mind.

We spend an enormous amount of time and energy preparing for one holiday, and often save for months too, so that we have a few days away from our homes, with people we don't know, to watch the rain over a different set of rooftops. Holidays are meant to be happy times, yet people often argue and are miserable, perhaps because they are in unaccustomed close proximity with one another, and in unfamiliar surroundings. But I'm quite sure that, if God needed to take a break, then certainly so do we.

We actually need a change in routine — not too far or for too long, mind, we need to know that we'll be coming back — but we need to vary the pace so that we can find out a little more about ourselves, each other and God. Like all the other celebrations, holiday is an opportunity to come aside from life and look at it from a different angle. A holiday is a chance to see what it's like to be different — so often townies make for the country and desk-sitters walk, or swim, or ski for miles. When I'm working I usually dress quite formally and always wear make-up, jewellery and perfume. On holiday I am the most messy person on the beach – no make-up, no jewels, or perfume, old clothes which I get out year after year despite my children's screams of hysterical laughter, and most important of all, no watch. For me, a holiday, or even my day off, is a chance not to live by the clock, whose demands follow me relentlessly every other day of the year. As long as I know when dinner (cooked by someone else, of course) will be served, I just don't want to know what the time is.

Neither do I especially want to see sights, of any sort. I like to be near the sea – I expect that's because my childhood holidays were always seaside ones – but as long as there's a modicum of sunshine, an assortment of drinks, some music in the background and a vast selection of reading material, I am more than satisfied. For me, a holiday is essentially a rest from everything – except my family, of course; I can't imagine a holiday alone.

When we take a break or a rest, we do a variety of things. Ideally we spend some time on loving ourselves, spoiling ourselves a little, and doing literally as WE please. Perhaps we feel that others "should" take that responsibility, but it's hard for them to love us if we're not very good at loving ourselves. Sometimes I say to a newly bereaved widow, "Behave towards yourself as you would if it were your next-door neighbour who had been bereaved. You'd be kind to her, make a bit of a fuss of her, and you wouldn't expect too much. You wouldn't say to her, 'Come on, snap out of it, cheer up', would you? You'd treat her gently and try to let her mourn in her own way, and at her own pace. Well, that's how you can be towards yourself."

But, we all need to take care of ourselves a little — not in a totally selfish way, of course, but to feel that we are worth it. And part of taking care is taking a break, literally "re-creation", taking an opportunity to let jangled nerves relax, and weary minds idle over nothing more important than whether to have vanilla or strawberry icecream. And it's when we slow down that, sometimes, things float to the surface — maybe ideas, maybe hurts, maybe old memories that we thought had gone.

Sometimes, too, it's at these moments of quiet that God speaks to us. Jesus had gone away himself one day, to a "lonely place" and a large crowd had followed him, desperate for good news and healing. The Bible says that Jesus felt sorry for them because "they were like a sheep without a shepherd", and that he talked to the people and healed those who needed it (Matthew 14:13–21; Mark 6:30–44; Luke 9:10–17; John 6:1–13). The people were tired and hungry, and the disciples were all for sending them into villages — perhaps miles away — to buy themselves food. But Jesus didn't want them to go away, and told the disciples to give the people something to eat. The disciples were dismayed — they certainly hadn't enough money to buy food for everyone. Andrew found a boy with a packed lunch (and I'll bet it was his mum who packed it), but that was only a very small amount. Jesus said, "Make the people sit down", and then he was able to make a miracle, and feed the whole crowd, with food left over at the end. After an exhausting day, Jesus then sent the people away, and went off to a quiet place himself, presumably to rest and recuperate.

It seems amazing that the Saviour of the World, the Son of God, should worry about a crowd of people being hungry. I doubt very much whether they would have starved if they'd missed that one meal – indeed, Jesus might have considered it a sort of sacrificial act, to make the day something different. I expect that if Jesus had asked the people to deny themselves that meal, and to go home hungry, so that the message of the day could sink in better, many of them would have complied. But then what would they have remembered of that day? What would be the first thing they told their family when they got home? What nice stories Jesus had told? The fun they'd had? The people who'd been cured? I don't think so. I think that the word on everyone's lips would have been the fact that he'd sent them home hungry, and their families would have thought how odd it was, and might have thought twice about going to see Jesus next time, if he went in for those strange practices.

I once went to a wedding which was, in every possible respect, quite beautiful – gorgeous bride in a superb dress; men in top hat and tails; a picturesque church with choir and bells; meal in a rustic restaurant by a river, followed by a dance on the lawn. Yet what I always remember most about that day was that the groom's brother and the bride's father had a fight. It was quite brief – but spectacular of course – and *that* was what I told everyone when I came home!

But Jesus did, I think, care genuinely about the

crowd's physical comfort, and provided a miracle in a most positive and engaging manner. St John is the only gospel writer who reports that the people noticed the miracle, for which perhaps St John had his own reasons. I would think it more likely that the crowd didn't notice anything at all out of the ordinary, but just got on and ate gladly. I don't think Jesus made a fuss about what he was giving, and it seems that he was happy to serve the people himself.

Jesus made them sit down first, they had to be passive and allow him to serve them, and to give them all that they needed.

Sometimes it's not until we sit down that we are aware of the miracles going on around us. It's not until we take a break that we notice the sunshine on our children's hair, or how big and powerful the sea is, or how nice it is to walk along arm in arm with our loved ones. We may also realize an answer to a problem that's been bugging us, but while we were busy there was never any time to look at it from a distance. Then sometimes, being just slightly away from our everyday life, a new idea is suggested which would benefit us, our neighbourhood or community, and we can try to make something similar when we get back.

I know too that, sometimes, stopping and taking a break makes us realize how awful things are. People who are recently bereaved say, "I'm all right as long as I keep going", but in a sense that is to avoid the pain – through which, at some time, we must necessarily go. Sometimes we use busyness to excape from hurt feelings, and "throw ourselves into our work", but I'm sure that the pain will make itself felt one way or another, in order that it may be resolved. It doesn't go away if not dealt with, it simply festers in an uncomfortable lump, waiting to emerge as an illness or a breakdown when we least expect it. Sometimes a minor disaster is the gap through which it bursts – we know the situation where someone copes magnificently through a major disaster, then absolutely collapses when a cup gets broken.

There are times too when we can "use" a relaxed situation; emotions might be overwhelming when it's our big event, while the slightly less close happening, at which we can relax, feels safer. My friend Jane's father died quite suddenly, and she was obliged to attend a large funeral at which she, obviously, was one of the main figures, together with her mother and sister, up at the front of the church. She was very conscious of lots of strangers looking at her, and of the need to support her mother, and felt numbed by it all. Three months later, Jane's husband's grandmother died. This time, Jane was not at the front, in the public eye, and, though fond of the old lady, had not been very close to her. Jane was amazed at how upset she was – but realized that actually she was "using" Nan's funeral as a time of mourning for her father. The distance had allowed her to do that.

God needed to stop after six days' hard work. We too need to stop after hard work, to come aside from our regular routine, and consider and think and meditate and tread water a bit – especially those whose work is constant service and giving of themselves, although they, of course, are the ones who are worst at taking time off. There is a sort of heroism about going for burn-out which actually does no one any good. These people speak with pride about not having had a day off for three weeks, or not having spent an evening at home for a fortnight. I wonder what they're trying to avoid? If they are their own worst enemies, perhaps it is themselves.

The fact is, that if we stop, we might not like what we find. We might not like ourselves. We might find ourselves at the mercy of our emotions, and feel out of control. The thing about work is that we are always in control, because, in the end, we can always stop when it gets too much. The jumble sale that is our own emotions, however, is still there every time we go back for another peep. But, until we can accept the mess that is ours, we can never really help with anyone else's.

In the quiet of a holiday, or a break, or a day off, we recognize our vulnerability. How foolish we were to think we were tough and strong. And it's not until we sit down and recognize our own needs that we realize that God is not only there with us, but actually feeding us himself.

All we have to do is sit down at the table.

Nine

September

"God will put his angels in charge of you to protect you wherever you go"

(Psalm 91:11)

September is my favourite month — not just because it's my birthday then, but because I really think it's a beautiful time of the year, and full of such wonderful colours. There are still plenty of flowers about, but the leaves are beginning to lose their sharp, busy greenness in favour of a gentler, mellower auburn. The ripening fruits catch the sun's rays and give back their fragrance in return. The mornings and evenings are a little cooler, but the daytime is gloriously warm and not quite so dusty as July and August. Because the school year has dominated so much of my life, I still see September as a new start, with all sorts of exciting potential ahead.

September is also the time for the feast, on the 29th, of St Michael (the Archangel) and All the Angels, and, for me, if ever a month were to be angel-filled, September it is. (I know that angels reach the peak of their public popularity around Christmas, because of their important place, mainly as God's messengers, in the nativity story, but I believe them to be around all the time.

There is evidence of a belief in some sort of angelic being at least as far back as Sumerian times, 3500 years before Jesus, when pictures of human-type beings with wings were etched on the walls. In the

Old Testament of the Bible there are many references to angels — "an angel of the Lord" often comes with a message from God. Sometimes people didn't recognize them as such, so we can only assume that they looked like ordinary people. At other times, though, "glory shone around" and their appearance was so startling that people were frightened. Jesus often referred to angels in a sort of administrative capacity as in "the angels will go out and gather up the evil people from among the good" (Matthew 13:41), and "he will send his angels to the far corners of the earth, and they will gather his chosen people" (Matthew 24:31), or guarding his tomb — "she (Mary) saw two angels there dressed in white" (John 20:11). There are lots of carvings of angels in churches, and they are often featured in classical paintings.

I think that they are not always quite as substantial as those chubby-chopped cherubs that you see on Christmas cards, nor the solid, still, stone angels who guard graves in our cemeteries. I think that they're often more like a floating leaf, or a ray of sunshine, or a rainbow. I read once that it is lucky to catch a leaf as it falls from the tree, and that, if you do, you should make a wish. While that, as it stands, might be called superstition or folk religion, the idea that a sudden, unexpected blessing should fall upon us, and reveal to us something of God's love, is theologically sound. That's what angels do. They point us to a truth about God. We may not notice what attracts our attention to it — an imagined sound, or a slight fluttering caught out of the corner of an eye, is just enough to by-pass our reasoning mind and go straight to our feeling heart. An idea comes to us; we remember a beautiful moment, or our mood is changed, perhaps calmed or quietened. That's the work of the angels.

I don't think that angels ever stab us in the back, or do wicked things – though the Bible mentions that "even Satan can disguise himself to look like an angel of light" (2 Corinthians 11:14) – but sometimes they may be cheeky. The man who used to carry the candles in procession at my old church reckoned that it was an angel who once blew the candle so that it set fire to his hair. It's nice to think of angels as cheerful beings, who like to play, and I have found it a helpful idea to imagine that babies who have died go to heaven to be made angels – or cherubs, should I say? The hierarchy is a bit complicated. I know that the seven archangels are in charge of the others – Uriel, Raphael, Raguel, Michael, Saraquel, Gabriel and Remiel all sound suspiciously masculine names, except when my son misheard, and asked about the "Archangel Muriel"! Jesus said that angels do not marry (Matthew 22:30), but other than that, a great deal of detail is left to our imaginations.

Lots of people like to think of angels as guardians, sent by God to watch over us, but I wouldn't want to lose the idea of God's presence always with us, in God's Holy Spirit. Angels point us towards God, and the things that God wants us to see. Sometimes God uses people as angels, and just a word, perhaps even overheard in a conversation between other people, can enable us to feel a touch of God's love.

Although originally intending to go to university, I left school to train as a nurse which, for various reasons, was never really "me". I helped in a butcher's shop, worked as an accompanist for music lessons in school, and helped my mother in her accountancy work. I even did a course in drama, vaguely thinking that one day I might teach – unfortunately the training college which I had intended to go to was shut down, and I discovered that I didn't like children very much (en masse, that is – I do like mine – really). I felt very despondent, and didn't know what to do with the rest of my life. Then I went on a diocesan day of celebration, when thousands of people converged on a disused airfield, to meet together and worship. As far as I could see, the day was a disaster. It poured with rain and there were about four ladies' toilets on the campus. I spent all day queuing in the rain, either for me or one of the children to go to the toilet.

While I was waiting in the final queue before we went home, a lady walked past with some papers over her arm. The back one, which I could see, read "Women's Ministry in the Church of England". I asked my friend to mind the children for me while I dashed off – somehow I felt I must have that pamphlet. I asked the lady where she got it, and arrived at the stall as the women's work adviser was putting everything away. The pamphlet was 10p and I had no money, so the adviser told me to read the pamphlet, and a few other, similar ones, and then come to see her in a couple of weeks' time. As I read the pamphlets, on the way home in the coach, I knew what I'd been waiting for. There was no Monty Pythonesque hand coming down from the sky – just an angel walking past with that pamphlet where I could see it. She might have had another at the back of the pile, or she might have put them in her bag, but I believe that God wanted me to see that, so that I was pointed in the direction He wanted me to go. Unfortunately, I cannot tell whether it really was God calling me – and I've no doubt that some would be quite sure that it wasn't and couldn't have been – because I cannot test my vocation as far as I would like to – to the priesthood. But what could be better preparation for ministerial training than nursing and drama? It seemed to me that God had made a sense out of the jumble sale of my life by showing me the next path to try, and had used a person as an angel to show me the way.

I'm sure that God uses colours as angels too, as they can be so influential in our lives, often subliminally. Ever since I was a child, I have thought of things and people as colours. Days of the week, for example: Monday is pale grey; Tuesday is apple green; Wednesday is salmon pink and Thursday is purple; Friday is emerald green; Saturday is red and/or turquoise; and Sunday is golden yellow. My friends will tell you that I loathe yellow, and never buy anything in that colour – so I don't know what that says about Sunday!

Sometimes I think I can see an aura of colour around a person – those I like tend to be green, red or pink – those I'm not so keen on, blue or grey.

I'm also very influenced by smell, and would find it hard to eat or drink something that didn't smell "right". As I go round to visit people's homes I reckon to feel comfortable or otherwise according to the smell there, and for each of us our home has its own special fragrance. I used to work on a television worship programme called "This is the Day" (BBC TV), and I had to go all over the country, as the worship takes place where people are. Perhaps one of the most interesting places I visited was a prison – and they have a smell all of their own – where a man who was nearing the end of a very long sentence had come to the faith, and was kind enough, and brave enough, to talk about it on television. While we were waiting about before the programme, the man, who was called Mel, told me about the preparations that he was making for his release. His first step had been to go out for a ride in a car, just for half an hour or so, but not far down the road, he found the smell of petrol fumes over-whelming and felt ill, and had to ask to be taken back to the prison. The next step had been to spend a day with his family, which went very well. He'd had a very happy day, but wasn't prepared for his niece to hand him her new baby. Mel said, "I just sat there with tears streaming down my face – it was the smell." And as he said that, for a moment I was taken back to that warm, milky perfume of a baby.

It's funny that something that we can't see, and that is, according to my scientist brother-in-law, extremely difficult to "quantify", should be so powerful. Think of hospitals, and what comes immediately but that evocative mixture of polish, boiled cabbage and disinfectant? Think of church, and the pungent mixture of musty hymn-books, candle wax and incense comes instantly to mind. Grandmothers seem to have a smell all of their own too – it used to be Pond's Vanishing Cream and Yardley's April Violets, but I think these days it's more likely to be a "power-dressing" perfume and decaffeinated coffee or herb tea!

We have become so used to being bludgeoned over the head by consumer information in the media that we sometimes don't notice the much more subtle messages that God sends to us via the angels. There are no miraculous answers, no stupendous announcements or detailed instructions, but instead a hint, a whiff, of something bigger and deeper than ourselves, a momentary reminder of our origins and our destination. The angels tell us that God is with us, and supporting us all in a hand which is, at the same time, big enough to hold the world, and small enough to touch a heart. The angels, in all their guises, help us to see what is invisible, and feel what can't be touched; the angels bring God's message that we are chosen, delighted in, forgiven and loved.

Ten

October

"What does the Lord require of you but to do justice, love kindness and walk humbly with your God"

(Micah 6:8)

Fig. 157: The good Samaritan (10:30–34).

I've heard people say that the three essentials of life are 3S's: sustenance, shelter and sex, but certainly the second two without the first would be pretty useless. You'd end up eating your home, and I don't think you'd feel much like sex. Food and water are absolute everyday essentials without which we die, so it's no wonder that primitive peoples sacrificed large quantities of food to their gods by burning it. It shows most devotion to give away something you really need, and how better to donate it to an invisible being than to turn it into rising, vanishing smoke? The instructions are all there in the book of Leviticus, with plenty of gory detail.

I've no doubt that, after a while, the people recognized that, no matter how many bulls they sacrificed, in some years the harvest was better than others. They had, of course, put all their efforts into meeting the sacrificial requirements, and, it seems, saw little connection between their ordinary lives outside the Temple and what went on inside it. The later prophets pointed to all sorts of double-dealing and fiddling the books, and in an Old Testament description of inflation, which rings bells with us now, Haggai talked of "earning wages to put them into a bag with holes" (Haggai 1:6). The prophets often warned the people around them that they were missing the point: God did not want ever more elaborate sacrifices, but that the people should "do justice, love kindness and walk humbly with your God" (Micah 6:8). It wasn't until Jesus came along that people began to get the idea.

Harvest is a festival when we celebrate God's concern with our most basic needs. We give thanks to God for our food, the "soft refreshing rain", and all the other gifts that come from the earth around us. It is an opportunity to remember our dependence on God's goodness, and to recognize that, no matter how hard the farmers work, or how thoroughly they support their work with scientific discovery, in the end it all depends on God and the earth's own rhythms.

Usually, if you go into a church at harvest time, there is a magnificent display of food, especially fresh fruit and vegetables. (It was from just such a display that Ben, then aged about eighteen months, chose a rosy apple and started eating it, while I was busy receiving communion!) Sometimes an imaginative group will add fish – the harvest of the sea; coal – the harvest of the deep earth; and wool – the harvest donated by sheep. But really, however high we piled the display on the altar, it would only ever be a small part of the thanks which we owe to God. So the display is a sacrament – an outward, visible sign of an inward and invisible acknowledgement that, without our food, we would be no more.

It is just as well that we are not fed according to merit or according to how grateful we are, but because God is good. The sun rises on evil and just alike, and the harvest is not dependent upon the farmer's personal morality. When Jesus healed the lepers (Luke 17:11) *all* were cured of their disease, and the nine who rushed off just as well as the one who came back to say thank you. When we say thank you to God, at harvest-time, we thank God for the generosity, reliability and love that is showered upon us – and all quite undeservedly.

But then we are forced to remember those many people, almost two-thirds of the world, who, just as undeserving as we, go hungry. We might ask how such a situation as we see, say, in Ethiopia, can possibly bear out our worship of an all-loving, all-caring God. Why is it that we should stockpile butter and throw away tons of food each day, when people are walking for miles to find a bowlful of rice, while their families die of starvation around them. There is no doubt that human greed causes endless problems, but it does seem, too, that parts of the world are, in themselves, much less able to be farmed in any sense of the word. However, we have seen that, in some places, the introduction of simple techniques, of irrigation, for example, make all the difference, and there are organizations who specialize in putting into practice the theory that to give someone a fish is to feed them for a day, while to teach someone how to catch fish is to feed that person, and others, for a lifetime.

Our thankfulness to God is shown not only at harvest time, but all the year round as we use the gifts that we have been given. In our responsible use of our blessings and resources we can demonstrate our gratitude to God in the way that God likes best, making sure that all God's children are cared for. The sad fact is, of course, that so many people go hungry because of the carelessness of their sisters and brothers. Most people in the West eat far too much, making obesity a major cause of death, and eat things which not only aren't good for our bodies, like lots of red meat, but which use up so many more resources in their production. The grain that is used to make animals tempting to their eaters, and lucrative for their killers, could be feeding human beings, to the advantage of them – and, of course, the animals.

As countries, we worry about spending money on defence, sometimes building weapons which are unusable, while taking huge sums of money as interest from third world countries which will be for ever in debt unless something radical is done. Jesus often talked about giving, and suggested, for instance, that we should "sell all your belongings and give the money to the poor" (Luke 12:33); also "when someone asks you for something, give it to them" (Matthew 5:42); "you have received without paying, so give without being paid" (Matthew 10:9); "There is more happiness in giving than in receiving" (Acts 20:35), and so on. I think that part of our thankfulness to God should be our willingness to give generously and gently. I understand that in parts of India, if you give some money to a beggar, you are supposed to say "thank you" to him or her, for allowing you the opportunity to give.

Sadly, the whole idea of sharing has been replaced by charitable giving, which is not the same thing. The former assumes that everyone has a right to an equal part of the resources and produce of the earth; the latter that it is the business of some people, who have the good fortune to have, to be able to choose to donate some of "their" possessions to others who don't have the same good fortune. This relies on human generosity, which is always unreliable. Few people are able to do as Jesus commanded, and store up their treasures in heaven (Matthew 6:20); most of us need the confidence and security which some treasures on earth can give us. But we all know the people who, no matter how much money they have, are still unhappy, and poor in spirit. Harvest time reminds us that the things God has given us are good and plentiful, but very much to be used and shared, not stored up.

Most parents have said to a child who won't finish its dinner – "Think of those children in Africa/India. Fancy leaving food on your plate when they are starving." Younger children are suitably impressed, and perhaps may be cajoled into finishing their food, but it's not long before some bright spark holds up the plate and says, "Here you are, mum, put it in an envelope and send it to them, if they're so hungry" – an example which demonstrates something of the complexity of trying to share the world's bounty. I've often worried about the wisdom of giving money to a charity to distribute on my behalf, or whether perhaps I should adopt a child in a foreign country, and send money direct to that family. I wouldn't want to appear patriarchal, but the thought of money going to a specific person, whom I could get to know a bit, is attractive. When I have talked about churches in inner city areas to people in richer climes, I have often recommended that the two groups get together to find out about all the things they have in common, as well as how they can help each other.

Harvest time gives us a special opportunity to put

our thanksgiving into practice, but we have to be careful not to focus all our thanksgiving into one weekend. The word "Eucharist" means "thanksgiving", and we can offer our thanks to God in church and at home regularly and with feeling, especially when something good has happened. Worship is one long drawn-out "thank you" which extends into every part of life, even the parts that "thanks" has difficulty in reaching. It's nice to hear people say "Thank God!" in ordinary conversation, even if they say it more as a figure of speech than as a prayer. I try to make a point of saying it, as a sort of witness that people can pick up if they like. My mother always has a very easy, natural way of talking about God-things, and I think that to follow her example is a good way of surrounding and supporting the family with praise and prayer, without it feeling artificial or forced. Then when something happens – a beloved cat dies, or granny becomes very ill – the simple explanation in faith-terms is acceptable and helpful.

I was brought up to say my prayers each evening, and until I was about ten, one or other of our parents said them with us. I continued the practice with my children, and re-introduced the grace after our main meal. We have always said grace *after* the meal – I'm not sure why – perhaps because, as one of my children suggested, by then you know what you're thanking God for, and how much you mean it! In fact, grace is the only prayer we say together as a family these days, and I'm glad that we still do, even though the children are grown up. My daughter Katy once devised a "Pentecostal" style grace which involved much clapping and hilarity, which was fine until, in their fervour, someone knocked over a bottle of ketchup, so we went back to the old-fashioned "Thank you God for my good dinner. Amen."

I often suggest to families that grace is a good prayer to start with, as we quite normally teach children to say "Thank you" or "Ta" before they can possibly understand the idea, in the hope that they will learn to become grateful. Similarly, if we, as God's children, most of us in extreme infancy, regardless of our earth-age, can learn to say thank you to God, we may absorb the concept until it becomes part of us.

When I started work as a minister, my vicar gave me a long list of people to visit, including a charming couple who lived quite near the church, and had expressed an interest in it but had never actually come to a service. They were very welcoming and friendly, and we enjoyed a cup of tea together. I eventually got up the courage to ask if they would be coming to church soon. The woman said, "Well no, you see, we're very lucky, we have good jobs and a nice home and lovely families – we don't need to come to church. We would come if we were in trouble at any time though." I congratulated them on their good fortune, and suggested that they might like to come and say thank you for it. I'm so pleased to say that they did come, and they discovered that being thankful can make life even better.

Eleven
November
Saints and Fireworks

Some people see the month of November as a sad and empty month. They see the leaves, burning colours gone to dark dampness, rotting away on the ground and blowing about in the wind and rain. A solitary rose, dirtied now, looks incongruous in the winter clothing of the garden, like used confetti in an old churchyard. It's not near enough to Christmas to start getting excited, and the holidays seem a long time ago.

It's onto this rather gloomy backdrop that God projects a celebration of countless lives on All Saints Day (1st November); faces flicker onto the screen, fascinating us with their difference; women, men, old, young, black, yellow and white, the saints have nothing in common save their saintliness, and we can but wonder at that. An enormous number of saints are listed by name – James, George, Edmund, Angela – while many times that number are people whose special response to God's call was known only to God. I often wonder what Heaven is like, and how they get on up there – in human terms they haven't a lot in common. St Euthymius the Great, for example, lived at the turn of the fifth century; he was a Middle Eastern priest and monk who healed the paralysed son of an important sheikh. Would he have much to say to St Wilgefortis, a

Portuguese princess who was promised in marriage to the King of Sicily, but who, since she'd made a vow of virginity, prayed to God for help and soon began to grow a beard? (For a time, her name was invoked by women who had troublesome husbands.) I sometimes think, reading stories of the saints, that some of them are quite unattractive characters, with whom it must have been difficult to live. Others though, like Columba, who was loving to everyone and "happy-faced", and Frances of Rome, a laywoman, wife and mother, yet undoubtedly a religious power in fifteenth-century Rome, seem to have radiated warmth and were much sought after.

But what they all have in common is that, having been called by God, they responded to the call and remained faithful to him, so that, in them, a little more of God's purpose was fulfilled. They themselves were blessed in being chosen by God – though I suspect they weren't always delighted – and through them other people were blessed too. They were certainly human beings, however, and must have had feelings like the rest of us. For me, that makes not only the personalities of the saints, but also my own pursuit of saintliness, rather dearer to my heart. We can be strengthened by their continuing prayers for us in heaven, and encouraged by their real life example.

St Paul often addressed his letters "to the saints at . . .", and I think it's safe to say that we who are called to be Christians can count ourselves apprentice saints as well. Jesus gave us a rule for life in the Sermon on the Mount (Matthew 5:1–12), though unfortunately it's rather like the instruction leaflet of my new calculator – brief. The best way to find out how to use all the functions of the calculator is to use it every day; the same is so with life – we learn best by living it to the full, as best we can, every day, going back to the rules to check our progress.

Jesus said –

Blessed are the poor in spirit, for theirs is the Kingdom of Heaven.

Blessed are those who mourn, for they shall be comforted.

Blessed are the meek, for they shall inherit the earth.

Blessed are those who hunger and thirst for righteousness, for they shall be satisfied.

Blessed are the merciful, for they shall obtain mercy.

Blessed are the pure in heart, for they shall see God.

Blessed are the peacemakers, for they shall be called sons of God.

Blessed are those who are persecuted, for righteousness' sake, for theirs is the Kingdom of Heaven.

Blessed are you, when men revile you and persecute you and utter all kinds of evil against you falsely on my account.

Rejoice and be glad, for your reward is great in Heaven, for so men persecuted the prophets who were before you.

(Matthew 5:3–12; R.S.V.)

Some of these qualities are obviously saint-making.

In these days of assertiveness, meekness is not regarded as a quality to be encouraged, but what is worse than a person constantly blowing their own trumpet? There are times when we must sacrifice self, and best to do it cheerfully, constructively and with love. Sometimes this means simply being a listener. In these days, when we are blasted from every angle with noise, as information and advertising are imposed upon us, it is lovely to meet someone who wants to hear about us, allows us to talk, and is apparently enthralled by the pedestrian details of our lives. We need the listening saints.

We can also try echoing God's mercy. Thankfully, official condemnation is in the hands of a few, highly trained legal officials, but how intolerant and condemning we are every day, in attitude and conversation, about those who have erred and strayed, or fallen on hard times. We quite forget that "there but for the grace of God . . .", but then God's mercy is boundless, of course, a bold contrast to our limited, prejudiced minds.

Mercy is an essential part of the forgiveness process but one which becomes a bit tired if the one who is forgiven shows no change in attitude and behaviour. So at the same time we must cultivate a desire to do what God wants – in other words, to hunger and thirst after righteousness – which can be translated into action to bring about change. Apprentice saints are always on the move – not physically, necessarily, at all, but learning and growing towards God through the practice of prayer, meditation and loving. To use the very basic physical terms "hunger and thirst" is to help us to realize the way in which the growing comes from the depths of an everyday experience. We get hungry with monotonous regularity, eat, then get hungry again, and so it is with righteousness. We might work to put right one small error in ourselves or the world, and be pleased and relieved about it, but then we realize that that is but one small step towards the world that God yearns for, and we become hungry again. This all sounds very active, but I do not want to dismiss the importance of prayer and prayerful reflection, which even the most disabled person can do.

But I worry that so much of what we do seems minute in the whole scheme of things — how can a tiny gesture or prayer on my part be of any real use? Then I remember the kaleidoscope theory, provided by my friend, Monica Furlong. Sadly, when I wanted to preach about this, I had great difficulty in buying a kaleidoscope, and some of the children didn't know what I was talking about. It's a tube of cardboard or metal, with a small peep-hole at one end, and the other end opaque. At the opaque end there are small pieces of coloured glass and two mirrors, set at angles to one another, so that by holding the tube to the light, the pieces of glass make a pattern which is repeated again and again by the mirrors. The fascination is to move the tube around, so that the small pieces of glass change position, thereby altering the pattern — infinitely, I should think. Monica's idea is that, although we may think the contribution that we make to world peace and justice is insignificant, it changes the pattern of life and may have far-reaching effects. We recognize, though, that our hunger will not be sated in this life — unless, of course, the Heavenly Banquet comes here first.

I have agonized over the business of being "pure in heart" — surely the more we live the less pure our hearts become – assuming, of course (and, having had children, I'm not at all sure of this), that they were pure in the first place! I feel that the people I like and admire best are those whose hearts are battered and scarred with the efforts and pain of living real life to the full, with vigour and courage, and risks taken on all fronts. Perhaps it means those whose hearts move towards pure love, which may well cause them to be hurt, to fall and fail, and yet which also gives strength enough to get up and try again and again. There is something, too, about having pure motives, that what impels us is the love of God and the desire for God's commonwealth to be realized on earth. I find it hard sometimes to separate my own desire to be liked and needed from the desire to do what God wants. It's all too easy to assume that God wants the same as I do.

It's rather the same with trying to be a peacemaker – usually it's because peace would be nicer for me. For people to be at peace would indeed be nicer for everyone, but it would also demand something from all of us. When we are able to work for the peace of all people – the right to a home, food, freedom from oppression and free speech being just a few of the elements of real peace – we may recognize the beginning of peace in our own soul. But it's not by any means just a knock-for-knock arrangement, where those who do good, get good done to them. Terry Waite, a leading figure in negotiations for the release of Middle Eastern hostages, was taken hostage himself in 1987. Even if he doesn't think it, there are certainly many of us who have protested, "Why Terry? He doesn't deserve such a thing". We can only live in the sure hope that, as a true son of

God, Terry's Father-in-heaven is with him, and thus he knows peace in his heart.

We are left with the saint-factors of being poor-in-spirit, mourning and persecuted, and for those we can thank God. Being a saint is not about going out to do wonderful and newsworthy things; we can be saints when we feel down, when things don't go well, when we feel that perhaps God has gone on holiday. We are especially blessed when we risk mourning – which doesn't necessarily happen when we lose something or someone – and we plumb some of the depths of sadness, making ourselves vulnerable and recognizing our weakness. We can even be saints when we are persecuted – not in quite the same way, perhaps, as saints of long ago, but when we have to hold out for something we believe to be right, when it's not the way of those around us. It is at these "down" times, when we feel we can't pray, that our membership of the company of saints comes to the rescue. Firstly, in that all those whose prayer is never silent, led by our brother and advocate, Jesus, are praying for us; and secondly, that even in our worst moments we are still part of that heavenly corporation. Our Lord and the saints having been real people here on earth can appreciate our efforts and our despair – they can even understand and accept our anger too, when, soon after the rosy glow of All Saints Day comes Fireworks Day.

We have come a long way from the historical situation which started this celebration on 5th November, and I suspect most of us have only a very hazy understanding of the Gunpowder Plot. However, Fireworks Night is big business, and in the face of increased concern for safety, is becoming an opportunity to get a party together and share in the fun – and the expense. Together we can be frightened at the noise and the flashes of light, which remind us only too well of flashes of temper and anger, which are part of our normal human emotions. Jesus was angry, we are told, at various times in his life, usually when someone was being exploited. "Jesus was angry as he looked round at them, but at the same time he felt sorry for them because they were so stubborn and wrong" (Mark 3:5). That was when the people were complaining that Jesus healed a man on the Sabbath. We are told (Matthew 21:12, 13; Luke 19:45–48; John 2:13–22) that Jesus got angry with people who were turning worship into big business at the Temple, and he actually allowed his anger to become physical, turning over the money-lenders' tables.

For a long time Christians, especially women, have been told that anger is wrong, and have been riddled with guilt at feeling irritated with other people, or occasionally even losing their tempers. Anger has been smothered, or even denied, which leads inevitably to problems. Anger is a God-given emotion which leads people to right wrongs and to crusade against evil; it is a force without which apathy wins and evil triumphs. However, I am not here endorsing a toddler's (or anyone else's for that matter) temper tantrum when (s)he can't have what (s)he wants. Neither is there an excuse for violence, which can only ever be degrading to humanity. But there is a place for indignation and a desire, born out of a concern for justice, to put things right, and bring a true order out of chaos. Our anger needs always to be scrutinized — which means, I think, that there is no opportunity for lost tempers, as that is always done on the spur of the moment, and counting up to ten, or whatever other way you choose, may save a whole lot of heartache and pain.

Some people see anger as an unnecessarily "over the top" emotion, but I think that one quality which unites the saints is the ability to go "over the top", in one way or another. To die for one's faith is the ultimate example of extravagance, but other saints have been extravagantly generous or extravagantly brave. I am all for extravagance, preferring feasting or fasting to dieting any day. The woman who anointed Jesus with Chanel-No. 5-equivalent (Matthew 26:6–13; Mark 14:3–9; John 12:1–8) was extravagant with her affection and her perfume, and we, as trainee saints, need to eschew a too careful regard of our behaviour or of our possessions.

To become a saint, we need to live life to the full, wherever that takes us, to pursue peace, to give, to be ourselves — only such absoluteness is enough to offer as thanksgiving for the ultimate extravagance of the one who gave his LIFE for us.

Twelve
December
"Good news . . . which will bring great joy to all the people"
(Luke 2:10)

I spent most of my childhood as a Methodist. Although baptized Anglican, when my parents bought their own home the nearest Sunday School was at a Primitive Methodist Church, and so I was sent there. I became a Sunday School teacher, and played the harmonium and the piano with great gusto for all the choruses and hymns which are sung in at least four-part harmony as a matter of course in the Methodist Church. When we were about seventeen, some of my friends became members of the church, but I didn't want to. Somehow it didn't feel right for me.

By then I was in the sixth form at school, and our religious instruction lessons were often discussions on religion and politics. One day a friar came to lead our discussion, and told us that his main job was praying, which seemed most peculiar to us, and quite a waste of time. However, my mother had not long been diagnosed as suffering from multiple sclerosis, so after the lesson, I collared this friar and asked him to pray for my mother, whose condition improved. I was so delighted that I decided that I must find the friar again, and went to the church where he worked, St Philip's, Plaistow, the Sunday before Christmas.

At High Street South Methodist, we'd been

celebrating Christmas for some weeks, so it came as quite a shock to find the church, modern and beautiful, but quite devoid of decorations, or, indeed, any sign of Christmas at all. (Incidentally, the service was solemn evensong, and, though completely mystified with the prayer book, the chants and the business of kneeling, genuflecting and crossing one's self, I was utterly enchanted by the whole scene.)

This was my first introduction to Advent and the keeping of it as a liturgical season, and the idea is something that I've tried to hold on to ever since. For the start of the Christmas season gets earlier and earlier, so that Christmas Day becomes the *end* of the celebrations, rather than the beginning, and we don't really appreciate the readings and themes of Christmas and Epiphany (the time directly after Christmas), when everything has been put away for weeks and it's all over. Anyway, if we attend parties before Christmas, and then keep the season after it, we get the best of both worlds.

Seriously though, it is good to try, during December, to think of the time before Christ. We go back to the earliest stories in the Bible; stories of Abraham and Moses which tell of God's promises to the people of Israel. We hear how the prophets foretold a Messiah, and how John the Baptist announced his arrival. We hear again, usually the Sunday before Christmas (which, though refreshing our memories, rather diminishes the impact of waiting nine months), the story of the angel's announcement to Mary, and her decision to comply with God's wishes: "Be it unto me according to thy will." We can catch something of the anticipation, the anxious hopes and fears that were around in those days, telescoped into four weeks' worth of readings.

I have never held with the idea that things are more enjoyable if you have to wait for them. Usually, my imagination works overtime, and the real thing never quite lives up to my expectations. I'd much rather have a surprise. However, a period of preparation is something quite different, as, properly done, it enhances our use and enjoyment of the event, or gift, when it comes. Thus, to prepare for a holiday means that we take with us the things that we'll want, and we really appreciate the break because we don't spend ages worrying about the things we haven't done at home. Similarly, to prepare our hearts and minds for Christmas means that we imagine life without Jesus, and thus understand something of the impact that his coming made on world history and on our own little lives. This was the Christmas present beyond price – the Gift of gifts.

I'm not pretending it's the easiest thing to do, this preparation of ourselves, while everyone is going mad around us, and the round of Christmas parties begins. Not only that, but most of us have preparations to make for the festival – food to buy and prepare, cards to write and presents to choose. However, if we can just hold a little bit back until the big day – put the Nativity scene in position, but leave the baby out perhaps – it means that we notice the difference when He's there. The carols are fresh, sweet and very moving as we sing them at Christmas, round the crib. At last we can open the chocolates and the nuts, and Christmas is a special time, rather than a wearing, soulless month.

Part of what makes Christmas special is the presents that we all give and receive. My mother, when she was small, would be given a book, a small doll, an orange and an apple. By the time I was a child, in the fifties, even ordinary working-class people gave quite large toys to their children – doll's prams and doll's houses, toy typewriters and, of course, "Meccano", the metal construction toy, was a great favourite. When my children wrote their (extensive) present lists recently, record-players, televisions and electronic keyboards were the order of the day – except for Ben, my middle child, who requested the price of a school ski-ing holiday in Switzerland!

I enjoy buying our gifts for most people. I like to shop, basically, and present-buying gives me an excuse to do so, ad nauseam. My hope is that the gift will please the recipient, show them that I care and, because I usually give things that I would like, show them something of myself – if only that I'm generous.

God had a problem with presents. Look at those Israelites. God created them, chose them as a people through whom his will would be revealed to humanity. God promised them a land of their own and led them towards it, spectacularly saving them from their captors at the Red Sea. God fed them food from Heaven, and they had water to drink which sprang from a rock – as if they needed convincing that God was with them.

Were they happy? Were they contented?

Were they 'eck as like! (as they say in Coronation Street). They were rather like the children, when they were smaller, ripping their way through stacks of exciting presents on Christmas morning, then turning round to say to me, "Is that *all* Mum?"

No, the Israelites still argued and fought, and mismanaged themselves so badly that they were overthrown and defeated by all sorts. By the time they got to their worst, it seems that only the prophets knew how to honour their agreement with God. They believed that God would one day send the ultimate proof of faithfulness, a Messiah, a Saviour, but the people weren't exactly holding their breath. Who wanted a Suffering Servant for a leader?

But God wanted to give something. Love always wants to give – but what gift, into such a melée? Something that would appeal to everyone, a gift above all gifts that would satisfy all human longing.

So God sent a baby.

This baby was sent to make the people happy – the promised Messiah, a crying, talking, sleeping, walking piece of God-with-us. Now *that* should show the people that God cared – cared so much about their soppy ways, and their sinful, stupid behaviour that repeatedly, almost unfailingly, fell short of the mark, that here was the perfect human being, not only to show them how to live, but to die for them too. To die, not because of anything he did, but because of our sins, so that eternal life would be on offer to us all.

And in so doing, God showed us something of the Divine-self, the sacred heart of God's love, made vulnerable for us.

The problem was, how to present this very special gift?

These days we'd expect an invitation to Buckingham Palace, at the very least, with our best clothes on. To a certain extent, we try to reproduce that with tinsel, silver and gold decorations, tree lights and special food. It's to remind ourselves what a special time Christmas is.

But God's gift came, not in a palace, but in a cattle-shed. No red carpet – rather, bits of hay and straw mixed with scraps of food and dung – a smelly, grubby place, I guess. (A certain amount of conjecture here, from an inveterate city-dweller.) Yet while I may never have been in a cattle-shed, I know that my life is not exactly shiny and clean, and every Christmas, and today, that's where Jesus comes to. He comes to our shame and our misery, and those parts of us which are poor, no matter how much money we have in the bank. He comes as vulnerable as a new-born baby, as uncritical and trusting, as ready to find a way into our hearts.

And how do we react when called upon to accept this Gift? If we were called to the Palace tomorrow, we'd think, "No – they can't mean me – they must have made a mistake", and indeed, although we may deserve medals, we don't merit eternal life as an award for services rendered. But that's just what God wants for us – happy memories of love shared, a vision of a future hope, and peace in our hearts, all our days.

It's a gift to make us happy; confident about ourselves as people, knowing that we are loved and cherished, every hair on our heads known. It's a gift to show us that, and how, God cares; that is, by coming alongside us in our situation. Maybe that's not so desperate for us – we who are so fortunate – but for our sisters and brothers in other countries, who are starving to death, or oppressed, it's essential to have that care to hold on to. God knows and cares about us all – we cannot be liquidated or hurt or taken hostage without God's knowing and caring. And that goes for grief and disappointment and loneliness in our everyday lives too.

In giving gifts to people at Christmas, we try to share in God's caring. Most of us nowadays try to make a special effort towards those who need extra care. Money is given to charities; lonely people are invited to join in the fun, and we write cheery greetings to people we haven't seen for years, to let them know we haven't forgotten our links with them. Christmas is a time for spoiling ourselves and other people, to remind ourselves of how we are indulged by our God. It is a time of extravagance to remind us of God's most extravagant gift of God's very self.

Yet agencies report that Christmas is a peak time for marriage breakdown and suicide attempts. People are sickened by the over-indulgence, and what they see as false, and forced, bonhomie. The media insist that everyone must be jolly, that families will love each other, and that silver-haired grandparents will be welcomed with open arms by their beautiful and successful sons and daughters, together with the right number of boy and girl children, all of them smiling fit to burst. The reality of being pushed together with people we don't particularly know very well, or even like much, is just too much to bear, and, as well as being fed up with them and ourselves, we feel failures because we're not living up to the image.

Some people put Advent calendars and little Nativity scenes on top of their television – where

I come from, that is the place of honour, normally reserved for framed photographs of loved ones. Perhaps we go wrong in two ways – firstly, we look at the television and imagine that that is the answer to everything, when we should be looking at the crib; and secondly, after Christmas, we put away the crib, as if we don't need it any more – but leave the TV in place, of course.

It's hard to recognize that so much of what we see on television is synthetic, carefully edited to produce something larger than life. The programmes themselves are often excellent – our mistake is in imagining that they depict reality. Of course, that's the way we'd like it to be – but life isn't like that. Life is actually much more like the crib-scene – an unmarried mother with a worried, confused father, miles from home, wondering who on earth will come through the stable door next. It's actually simple in its complexity – the crib says that the answer to life is in living it, and in looking to God, for an answer to the question not of "How did all this happen?" but of "What for?"

After our days or weeks of fun and games, we wrap up the paraphernalia of Christmas and put it away, when really, of course, the work of Christmas continues all year round. Being born is a very important moment in a person's life, but it's actually only one step of the journey. Jesus's birth was wonderful and miraculous, but it was the beginning of a life which saw hard work, difficult times and ultimately an untimely and gruesome death. Our celebration of Christmas is, in itself, a preparation for the rest of the year; a recharging of batteries and a return to the basic facts of life. That's why we return to our roots, and yearn for things to be as they always were.

God's gift of Jesus at Christmas is perfectly timed; it comes so that the shining message of Christmas, wrapped in real human packaging, can give us peace in our hearts, by showing us that God does care for us. In some quite unexpected ways Christmas can give us a glimpse of God's self, and, at its simplest and most wholesome moments, gives us the impetus to go forward, with God, into another New Year.